PEOPLE ARE TALKING

The following testimonials are from just a few of the many business owners whose lives and businesses have been affected by the principles in this book. They may all be contacted by writing us at Grow@CranksetGroup.com

Thank you for all that you do for 'us' small business owners. You are greatly appreciated!

—TRISH MOORE

Process Mapping has changed my life!

—LYRIC TURNER

Chuck, your willingness to speak the truth to us about our blind spots while reinforcing what we do well (along with just the right dose of encouragement and support) has, and continues to be, a huge blessing to us and our business.

—EDDIE DRESCHER

I'll continue to rave about you and your programs. I know business owners can truly benefit from your expertise.

—FUYIU YIP

Thanks for the great class on [lifetime] goals. I really got a lot out of it & for the first time feel I have a 'Big Why'! I'm gaining a lot of clarity!

—BILL COLANGELO

…I knew that I wanted to give something back to him, on behalf of all of us that have been recipients of the guidance, encouragement, and just good solid advice that he shares so selflessly…Chuck's personal motto is, 'Live Well By Doing Good.' Everyone who has been around him for any length of time soon learns how passionate he is about living this out…

—MEGAN MCDONALD

Chuck, what an incredible day at your Strategic Business Plan Workshop. I am excited that I learned how to create a powerful business plan system that will take my business to the next level now.

—DAWN EVINS

I can't tell you what a success mapping out our invoice process has been. Since doing the one with you I have added several others, to great effect. Can't thank you enough. Now, we want to map out the same process for our 6 other clients AND combine them all into one repeatable process.

—RIC REIFEL

...just a quick note as we begin the journey of the 90-day challenge to thank you for providing an opportunity for all of us to realize our dreams. I have already learned a lot...

—ERICA GARDNER

Making Money Is Killing Your Business

MAKING MONEY IS
KILLING
YOUR BUSINESS

How to Build a Business You'll Love
and Have a Life, Too

CHUCK BLAKEMAN

Crankset Group

PUBLISHING

10 9 8 7 6 5 4 3 2 1

ISBN-13: 978-0-9843343-0-8

Crankset Publishing books are available at special quantity
discounts to use as premiums and sales promotions,
or for use in educational or corporate training programs. For
more information, please email us at
Grow@CranksetGroup.com, or write to the Director of Sales:
Crankset Publishing
1324 Shadow Mountain Drive, Highlands Ranch, CO 80126,
or contact your local bookstore.

This book is printed on acid-free paper.

Cover and layout design by http://gb-studio.tv/
Layout by WESType Publishing Services, Inc.

Library of Congress Cataloging-in-Publication Data

Making Money Is Killing Your Business: How to Build a Business
You'll Love and Have a Life, Too / by Chuck Blakeman.

1. Entrepreneurship.   2. Success in business.   3. New business enterprises.
I. Title.   II. Making Money is Killing Your Business: How to Build a Business
You'll Love and Have a Life, Too   III. Blakeman, Chuck

LCCN: 2009912900

To my dear and patient wife, Diane,
my stable influence,

and our great kids,
Grant, Laura and Brie,
who all grew up much faster than I did.

Contents

Acknowledgments

It's appropriate that I'm writing this early on the morning of Thanksgiving.

As I mention in the forward, everything I know is a summary of what I have learned from other people. We all learn from one another and the best we can do is take all of that learning from the world around us, from our family, friends, business associates, and other leaders, and sum it up in a fresh narrative for a new time. *Making Money is Killing Your Business* is such a compilation. My life is a sum of all the people who have had an impact on me, and the practical nature of this business book is a result of all those influences.

I delayed writing the acknowledgements until right before the book was published because I know it is impossible to thank everyone who has helped me grow, and by extension, contributed to this book. My apologies to those of you who are not named. My deepest gratitude to you all for playing a part in chipping away the barnacles on this book and my life. You know who you are.

I'm grateful for a mother and father who built a wonderful family, covered with all the usual warts and some great strengths. This began the process of learning for me. And foremost for my wife, Diane, who has been my biggest source of ongoing strength, and guidance. She has done a masterful job of keeping me on the pavement over the years. She never promotes herself and the key role she plays in the lives of so many we work with, so it's my pleasure do that here. Thank you, Diane!

Our incredible kids, Grant, Laura and Brie, have all contributed directly to my life and also directly to the writing of this book. They are a great inspiration to me, and the proud dad comes out whenever I get to talk about them. Grant has also been my source for fabulous cover designs, layout designs, branding and websites, Laura is always my go-to person for lucid copywriting and great marketing copy, and Brie will always use her creativity to bring to life any illustrations I need.

I am also deeply grateful to John Heenan from Belfast, Ireland, who is my brother from another mother. He has been a continuous voice in my ear with guiding thoughts like "Chuck, God doesn't make junk, and He didn't make you to fail." John and his friend, Mort Murphy from Cork, Ireland are also directly responsible for getting me starting on the Seven Stages of a Business when they first presented me with their own Nine Stages of Business Development. And both of them traveled at different times from Ireland to Denver at their own expense to help me when I was floundering. They are shining examples of people who live in a world of abundance.

A few years ago John and I met halfway in Virginia where he introduced me to a collegial group of business advisors scattered up and down the east coast of the US and in Ireland that Art and Lisa Radtke had assembled under the name Team Nimbus. My nearly year and a half of meeting together with them on a quarterly basis contributed significantly to the concepts I use in Making Money.

From that early group thanks especially to Art & Lisa, Mort, John, Bill Davis (a wise soul), Jim Roman (a clear thinker), and Arnel Tanyag (a change agent and transformational warrior). And a very special thanks to Eddie Drescher who, along with John Heenan, continues as a sounding board and great source of encouragement, and an example of someone who is using his life to help transform the businesses of many others.

Some special long term friends who have both directly and indirectly guided me before and during the writing of this book; my dear friend Gary Bradley who has always believed in me when many others had thought I had lost my way; Donald McGilchrist whose clarity of thought and faithfulness has made him a rock for me and many others over the decades; Chip Toth who is unashamed to tell men he loves them and then actually demonstrate that he does; and Keith Dubay, a great journalist and writer, who allows me to be me in golf, beer, food, and even in my writing. Thank you for everything you all do for me and for others.

Here locally in Denver, Dawn Margowski was with me from the beginning of this crazy journey and her positive spirit and encouragement is always a breath of fresh air—thank you! Megan McDonald has been a raving fan of what we do and a real source of encouragement to keep influencing the lives and businesses of others. Carrie Roberts has transformed herself, her own business, and other businesses along the way and is a great and faithful friend to Diane and me. And Brian Rants has been a steady example of pushing forward toward the goal with his own life and in his leadership of the 1010 Project (www.www.the1010project.org/).

Many business advisors influenced this book significantly. Here in Denver, Dawn Margowski, John Nordlander, Susan Kildahl, Ted Mersino, Darin Ray, Jane Schaeffer, and a number of others working with businesses have all contributed to the ideas that make up this book. Many others nationally and internationally have had a big impact, most notably Eddie Drescher, Arnel Tanyag, John Heenan, Mort Murphy, Chip Toth, Lisa Radtke, Art Radtke and Judith Briles.

Caleb Seeling is a great copywriter who took on the big task of turning my first manuscript into something people could actually read. And so many people gave me regular feedback on the progress of the book that I will not remember you all—again, forgive me. Some who invested significant time in this process—Donald McGilchrist, Megan McDonald, Melanie Matthews, Bill Colangelo,

Keith Dubay, Doug Root, my brother Jim Blakeman, my sister Virginia Lenz and her husband Mark Lenz, Dru Shockley, Chip Toth, and many others. Thank you all for being willing to tell me when I was going left and should be going right.

A special thanks to Glenn and Mary Hobratschk, who graciously gave me the use of their home in a very special setting in the Southwest where I was able to write 60 percent of this book.

I believe we are all made to do something significant with our lives. I can say with confidence that all of those named and un-named who contributed to this book live in a world of abundance, not in a world of scarcity, and are making a difference by living significantly. Thanks for your examples to me and to the world around you in which you live so intentionally. May your Big Why be realized.

Foreword

A lot of people have told me that some of the principles in this book are things they've never heard before. In the case of Lifetime Goals I get the following comment all the time, "I've never been given permission to think that way."

Allow me to set the record straight. I've never had an original thought in my life and I'm pretty sure no one else has either. I once heard an artist say "The best artists are simply the best plagiarists." There is nothing new under the sun and when I hear people claiming they have an amazing new way of doing something that no one else has ever thought of, it usually turns out it was all just marketing.

I didn't discover any new ideas about business or life in order to write this book. The best anybody can do is rediscover existing good ideas that have been ignored for a bit, and repackage familiar ones in a new narrative that are more relevant for our time. My hope is that this narrative is fresh for you and brings some long forgotten ideas back to life. And for those ideas with which you are already very familiar, I trust this narrative will give you a practical and concrete way of transforming your business and your life that works for you on the ground and in the trenches of business.

This book is also not intended to educate you. I'm not a big fan of education; I get much more excited about learning. For me the difference is simple. Education packs more information into my head and learning transforms the way I do things. Education is knowledge-based, learning is transformational. *Making Money is Killing Your Business* was not thought up in an ivory tower using business theories and concepts so that I could pack more information into your head. You have way too much of that already.

Making Money was discovered and re-discovered many times in the process of starting, growing and building businesses myself, and helping others do the same. My clients and I are all using everything in this book to build businesses with passion that we can enjoy for decades. I trust that Making Money will not become a shelf-help book for you (one of those books that helps your shelf look good), but a well-used, scratched up, written-in reference manual for building your business.

One of the big re-discoveries of old truths for me was that a business is supposed to throw off three things for us, time, money and significance. But for some reason we only expect it to give us one: money. And because we focus on just making money, our business never gives back time or helps us have a significant impact in the world around us. We're too busy making money to get to the important stuff.

As a result everything is backwards. We build a business and take whatever lifestyle that business happens to throw off for us, which at best usually involves having money, but rarely a lot of time, and almost never significance. This isn't surprising because "he who makes the rules wins," and we too often let our business and the business world around us make the rules for us. Making Money was written to help us take hold of our business and re-make the rules in our favor so that our business finally becomes our servant to do our bidding, not the other way around.

I'm still not ready to say the Four Building Blocks of a business are really THE four building blocks. There might be five or six, but in many years of doing business, I have found that if I have these four things in place, the rest of a healthy business structure and necessities will flow from them. Most of the fundamentals of a business are obvious. When we start a business, a number of things come find us: marketing, business development, operations, accounting and a few others. But the Four Building Blocks do not come find us, we have to proactively go get them and invite them into our business. Successful business owners do just that.

Some have asked for more information on the finance and accounting side of the business because it is so critical to success. My response is that you should read Financial Intelligence for Entrepreneurs: What You Really Need to Know About the Numbers, by Karen Berman and Joe Knight, and then go get a great CPA. There is no need for me to reinvent the wheel they've already created. This book is focused on the Four Building Blocks that are less obvious but every bit as important.

In the final analysis I believe I really only bring three things to the business owners I advise— clarity, hope and risk. If we gain clarity about where we are and where we want to go, and a measure of clarity about the first few steps to get there, that gives us hope. Not hope in the modern sense of wishing, but hope in the correct sense of the word—believing with conviction that I can do it. And that kind of hope will allow you to take the measured risks you need to take in order to build a business with passion that gives you the lifestyle you always wanted. I want to change your hope from wishing to believing.

For the most part, adults don't learn unless we are disoriented from our settled and sometimes stale view of reality. It is my hope that this book will also challenge your understanding of conventional business wisdom, and reintroduce you to some long forgotten central ideas and practices that can transform your business and your life.

Please use this book to build a business that will serve you, not the other way around. Use it to build a business that will take you from survival straight through success all the way to significance. And do it with passion.

PART I

GET CONTROL
Conquering the Tyranny of the Urgent

No Business Owner Can Survive Making Money

1

We get what we intend, not what we hope for.

—CHUCK BLAKEMAN

Most business owners think their purpose in business is to make money. Surprisingly, it's not. *The business owner's purpose is to build a business that makes money.* These two things are worlds apart, and almost every business owner I work with is absolutely buried in trying to make money, which keeps them from ever making a lot of it.

Within a few weeks of the birth of our first child, Diane and I were already imagining and anticipating how it would be when he was all grown up, had graduated from college and was out on his own. We had these same conversations after the birth of all three kids.

At the writing of this book, two of them are out on their own and running their own businesses and the third will graduate from college this year. All three of them are adults now and are just plain fun to be around. We look forward to an afternoon, holidays and even a vacation with them because we get as much as we give.

Maybe Diane and I are weird. From the beginning we thought of our kids not just as kids, but also as adults in the making. We were very aware that at some point the great amount of personal time, emotion, and money invested in guiding our kids would eventually grow into more of a two-way street. We hoped that as adults, we could all invest in each other, help each other find significance with our lives, and simply enjoy each other for decades.

OUR BUSINESSES SHOULD GROW UP, TOO

Perhaps that perspective is why I see business differently than some people. I think businesses should grow up, too. I don't mean "it would be nice if it happened." I mean we should all, every one of us, expect our businesses to grow up and start giving back to us and to the world around us. We should assume that at some point our business would move from survival right through success to significance.

Nobody would argue with me that we should intend for our children to grow up, leave home, and become grown-ups we could enjoy for decades, but when was the last time we had a similar conversation about our businesses? It's normal for children to grow up, so why isn't it normal for businesses to do the same thing? Frankly, we're in charge of both of them at birth, and if you've had kids, you'll know that you've got more control over the maturity of your business than the maturity of your kids.

And yet most businesses never grow up. We spend decades changing the diapers in our business and reporting to the vice principal on a regular basis to get it out of detention. Twenty years after we print a business card we seem to be spending as much time, emotion, and money on our business as we did the day it was born. Why would we so eagerly anticipate the maturity of our children and never expect the same for our business? Shouldn't we expect to be able to enjoy our mature business for decades as well?

I believe the root of the problem is that the conventional view of business isn't ever going to allow us to bring it to maturity. It's hard to believe, but what the title of this chapter says is true. The very thing you THINK will make your business successful, a focus on trying to make money, is the very thing keeping you from being successful. You're too busy making money. No business can survive that.

It's not a play on words—it's a serious problem. You're simply too busy making money, or even worse, trying to and not doing so. Either one prevents you from making as much as you could, and most likely is stopping you from building a business that will ever grow up.

If you want a mature business you can enjoy for decades and that makes money while you're on vacation you might need a new view of business to get there. You might just need to regain the perspective you had when the business was born, and get back the passion that brought you into business in the first place. Either way it's likely you'll have to do a *businessectomy* on both your thinking and processes to take your business from survival through success and all the way to significance.

For years your business has trained you to focus on making money (and other unproductive distractions), and unfortunately when you look at other businesses you see that most of them are focused on making money, too. But average businesses all set a bad example for us. They are dangerously following each other, Lemming style, towards the money-making cliff. Lemmings in fact don't voluntarily jump into the water and drown, but, like many business owners, they take their cues from those around them and assume that it must be normal to at least hang around the cliff just because everyone else is doing it.

BE NORMAL, NOT AVERAGE—BUILD A BUSINESS THAT MAKES MONEY FOR YOU

The point? It's *not* normal to have a business that never grows up. It's clearly *average*; everybody's doing it, but it is definitely not normal. We'll discover what is normal in Chapter Three—for now you should understand that the few things you need to do to move from average to normal will probably cut deeply into your idea of how business is run. So let's start the *businessectomy*—let the healing begin!

TWO OPPOSING REALITIES

There is a good explanation for why we get stuck trying to make money and rarely get around to building a business that does it for us. Business owners are constantly fighting to balance two opposing daily realities:

The Tyranny of the Urgent vs. *The Priority of the Important,* and the struggle between them is something every business owner faces daily.

Almost universally we let the Tyranny of the Urgent keep us from paying attention to the Priority of the Important. If this describes you (you may not even know it), you will probably never build a mature business.

Let's take a closer look at each of these:

Tyranny of the Urgent	Priority of the Important
(Making money myself.)	(Building a business that makes money.)
Must Be Reactive	Must be Proactive
Hostage	Freedom

THE TYRANNY OF THE URGENT

The Urgent things in our business fly at us all day every day, causing us to be *reactive* and defensive as we hold the business together as best we can. We jump from one Urgent task to another, or worse, manage many tasks at once while gleefully calling ourselves "multi-taskers."

The Urgent things are tyrannical—they want to rule over us. Like small unruly kids, they scream and yell, poke and prod, and are relentlessly in front of us. We don't have to find the Urgent things—they find us and force us to become their loyal subjects. Over time we resign ourselves to the notion that this is normal because our business taught us to live this way and, besides, all the businesses around us seem to be doing the same thing. Welcome to the *Business Treadmill.*

THE TREADMILL OF MAKING MONEY

One of the most Urgent things pulling at us daily is the need to make money to cover today's bills. Think about it. The day you opened your business, the sign smiled back briefly before it turned into this evil ranting, throbbing voice yelling "I need money!" That great-looking office space, those shiny trucks, and that centrally located storefront very quickly turned into a relentless liability to your cash flow. And you soon realized that the "clear and present danger" is not having enough money.

So from the start, your business taught you to go in search of money. How did you get money? From clients. How did you get clients? From sales. You did sales, so you could get some clients, so you could make some money, because your business told you it needed it.

It didn't take long before you realized your new clients wouldn't pay you for just signing them up, so you actually had to deliver or you wouldn't get paid. Very early on, your focus shifted from sales to production, and as you delivered the goods and services, your clients finally paid you. Just in time, too, because the rent was due the next day.

But because you had been so busy producing, you didn't have time to go out and get new clients, and suddenly you realized you had nothing in the pipeline. So you were back out doing sales, getting clients, producing, getting paid, doing sales, getting clients, producing, getting paid, and so on. It's the treadmill of making money.

Over time you got so used to this pressure that even when it's no longer there, and you're making enough money to buy a hot tub and go on an unpaid vacation a few weeks a year, you never left this mode of business. You have forgotten the excitement of going into business in the first place and actually think the goal now is to make money.

See how your business has trained you? You and most of the business owners around you have been conditioned to just keep changing diapers for decades. And because everyone else is doing it, it seems normal and natural—the way it works.

> Over time you are so used to this pressure you have forgotten the excitement of going into business in the first place and think the goal is to make money.

But, it's a dead end.

And it's the biggest reason why most businesses never grow up. At best they get sold for their assets and the customer list thirty years later when the owner finally gets off the treadmill at "retirement" which, by the way, is a bankrupt Industrial Age notion that has been replaced by something a lot more fun and meaningful—more on that in Chapter Six. The Tyranny of the Urgent creates a business that is like a three-year-old that never matures.

THE PRIORITY OF THE IMPORTANT

In stark contrast to the Tyranny of the Urgent is the *Priority of the Important*. The Important things sit quietly and patiently in the corner and whisper, "I'm really Important. But you're right; taking care of me today won't make you more money right now. So I guess I'll try to nudge you again next week as you go flying by."

The Urgent things bully us into being *reactive*, but the Important things require us to be *proactive* because they almost never seem Urgent—things like thinking about what next month or next year should look like, what my business should look like at maturity, how my customers are responding to what I sell them, if my processes are as good as they should be, and "I really need to write down how we do this someday." We don't make money today doing those kinds of things, so they don't seem Important, and they're definitely not as Urgent as paying the bills.

By the way, I'm not saying focusing on the Tyranny of the Urgent won't make you money. That's part of the problem. I know plenty of people making millions who are totally focused on the Tyranny of the Urgent. But they're on a treadmill, too, and a few don't even realize it. Living in reaction to the Urgent can only bring me *Riches*, which I define as *money*, while attending to the Important things will bring me *Wealth*, which is ***the freedom and the ability to choose what to do with my time.***

Which do you want? Riches you don't have time to use, or Wealth that allows you to go on vacation while your business makes money for you on its own? If you focus on the Tyranny of the Urgent and save the Important things for "later," your best hope is that you will make money, and never as much as you could or should. But if you focus on the Priority of the Important now, you'll be on the road to real Wealth: freedom. And freedom is the best evidence I can come up with that you now have a mature business.

> Riches are defined as money; Wealth is the freedom and ability to choose what to do with my time.

LATER NEVER COMES

Jim Baylor owns Pacifica Automotive Repair. He used to live with a real bad taste in his mouth for employees—he is a great mechanic and had the toughest time finding anyone who could do it as well. He proved this to himself time and again as he burned through mechanic after mechanic.

After plenty of prodding, he finally relented to "wasting" a few valuable afternoons over three months, time he could have used to make money, to write down the simple processes and standards for how he wanted things done. These things were second nature to him, and writing them down didn't seem like a good way to make more money—like documenting how to breathe. But he did it anyway, and then he wasted even more time going through those processes with his mechanics to train them on the new higher and more consistent standards.

Jim now has eight mechanics working for him and his business is highly regarded for the quality of their work. Not surprisingly, Jim trusts that every one of his mechanics can get the job done as well as him, and a few even better. This was just one of a number of Important things Jim did that changed his business and personal life, and it put him on the road to building a mature business. Now when Jim's on his favorite island sipping Mai Tai's, he is confident the business is making money while he's not around. He's enjoying both his mature kids and his mature business these days.

MAKING MONEY VS. BUILDING A BUSINESS

The Tyranny of the Urgent keeps us focused on making money. The Priority of the Important helps us build a business that makes money for us. Don't get me wrong. You have to make money. Okay, not you, the business. The problem is that the business teaches us to use our own personal time to make money. This is also called bootstrapping, pulling a business up by its own bootstraps. If we sell a widget, we take the profits to buy two more, sell those and buy four more.

Unless you take big investment money up front, you're likely to be the one making the widgets in the early stages of your business. If you're *growing* into business by bootstrapping, you have to fight the habit of focusing on making money yourself. Being the principal producer in your business will almost certainly keep you from building a business that makes money while you're on vacation.

But you still have to pay the bills early on while figuring out how to get out of the producer role. To do that I used a simple concept called *dual tracking*.

DUAL TRACKING

If we see our kids as adults in the making, it reminds us to make decisions that will help them both now and when they are adults, a form of dual track thinking. In business, dual tracking is nothing more than figuring out how to satisfy both the Urgent (making money to pay bills) and the Important (building a business to maturity) with the same activities.

Here's an example. When I first started advising and mentoring other business owners, I was alone—the sole producer. To get clients, I started the Business Leader's Insight (BLI) Lunch that

> *Dual Tracking* satisfies both the *Urgent* and the *Important* with the same activities.

still meets every Tuesday more than two and a half years later. I needed clients, so I did this free (to me) lunch—everybody bought their own lunch off the regular menu. It was a great way to serve the business community with my experience and create credibility that might lead to clients. The easy thing would have been to focus on using the lunch to make money right then— lead the discussion, get clients, produce, get paid, then go do another lunch.

But I wasn't satisfied just making money from the BLI Lunch—I was on the hunt to find ways to build a business that makes money for me. I had the mindset from the outset that I wanted to grow a mature business. So for the couple weeks that I was recruiting and working on the first lunch, I was constantly asking myself, "How can I use this activity to build a business that makes money while I'm on vacation?" What I hit on wasn't all that eye-opening, but it was incredibly helpful.

I wanted other facilitators to do at some point what I do, to either have their own BLI Lunch or start speaking at mine. So I wrote a process—what I did to get the lunches started, how I recruited people, the attributes of a good restaurant for such a thing, how to encourage interaction, and how to create a habitual environment from which business owners would benefit. I also created a handout and a leader's guide for that first lunch discussion.

Writing all this down added a good 45 minutes of prep time for each lunch—not a ton of time—and I decided to do a handout and leader's guide for each lunch thereafter. Instead of just holding a lunch, I used that potential money-making activity to help me build a business that would also make money later.

Documenting the process of starting and hosting a lunch, as well as creating lunch-talk handouts every week, hasn't made me any money directly and I could have seen all this as a distraction. But now that I have facilitators and clients in other cities who are starting their own lunches, all I've had to do is hand them the process, the dozens of workshops I've already produced and provide general guidance. They can just follow the process, add their own fresh examples to the handouts, and jump right in.

Another simple way I thought of to make money later when I'm not around was to record the lunches. I now have dozens of them in the can for distribution on the internet either free to attract clients, or for a fee. We're also turning them into white papers and they've formed the basis of workshops and seminars I do. They have even helped me write this book. These lunches now make money while I'm on vacation.

Important things, like writing down processes, rarely make us money right away, but they almost always make us a lot more money down the road—more than anything we do today that is Urgent. If you can dual track them, then you've found the sweet spot.

Samantha and Cam Dewalt have owned a wholesale and retail window store for 22 years, doing a tidy $2.5 million per year in gross revenues and providing a nice lifestyle for themselves. They told me they were successful and quite happy with the 22 years behind them and the next 15 or so in front of them before they retired. But as we talked about what it means to have true Wealth (freedom), Samantha's face got tighter and tighter, and after about 45 minutes she turned to me and said quietly, "I'm so sick of this. It doesn't seem like we can ever truly leave for a few days. This thing [their business] is like a stone around our necks." 22 years later she was still investing as much time and emotion into her business as when it was born, and that's simply not normal—average, yes, but not "normal." It will wear you out, and it had worn her to the bone.

For the first time in 22 years they were now building a business, not just making money.

We got started that day helping them learn how to dual track. For the first time in 22 years they were now building a business, not just making money. A couple months later they lost their highly valued office manager. When I checked in a couple weeks after that, I asked Samantha how the new person, Jenna, was working out. She said, "In the past, it would have been six months of relearning by trial and error, which would have cost us a lot of money. But because of some of the simple processes we've recently put into place, we only had to sit with Jenna for a few hours over a couple days and she got this thing figured out." Jenna, who was sitting right there, smiled and pointed to the simple process map we had done for the original office manager and said "I'm doing great as long as I have this."

Samantha and Cam were on their way to building a mature business for the first time in 22 years, and they very quickly gained confidence that they would see it happen in the next couple of years, allowing them to actually enjoy their business for many more years to come.

These are just two examples of dual tracking. It's not about being clever or creative, but simply being committed to finding ways to use every money-making activity in your business to pay your bills and at the same time help you build a future business that will make money when you're away doing something else important to you.

It's critical to ask yourself, "How can I use this task to build a business while I'm on vacation?" Ask that every day of every activity in your business, and your business will change dramatically and begin to grow up. If you're only focused on the Urgent, you're business will never get to maturity.

TIME AND MONEY

One of the fundamental mistakes we make is to measure our business against itself instead of against what it provides to us as business owners. An acquaintance of mine knew a realtor who was one of the top five realtors in their state, bringing in over $800,000 a month in personal revenue. If you asked her how her business was doing, she would always use words like "great," "fabulous," and "wonderful." But when she was challenged to take a good hard look at her business in terms of what it did for her personally, it was another story.

She had been avoiding that analysis for a very long time and for good reason. Under that glamorous façade was a business that was consuming every moment of her life and negatively affecting her family. And after her marketing expenses, including TV, radio, print, and support team, her all-consuming efforts were only bringing her a net income of $75,000 or less per year. Her business looked great until it was measured against what it did for her personally.

Our business should be built so that it provides two basic resources for us: time and money. We focus a lot on how it could provide us money but rarely think of how it could provide time for us as well. And it is this separation of the two that keeps us from having enough of either.

BUILDING A MATURE BUSINESS

We have to stop measuring our business against itself. My definition of a "mature business" is from the point of view of the owner, not from the viewpoint of the business itself. It's the business owner's lifestyle that indicates the maturity of the business, not the revenue or growth of the business. A mature business has at minimum two attributes:

1. The business owner is not the *producer*—if he is, it's by daily choice and not because he *has* to.

2. Because of number one, the business makes money while the owner is on vacation.

If measured appropriately, our business will provide both time and money for us, and the best proof of that is that it continues to make money while we're on vacation. Beyond this, business maturity can include a lot of things (see Chapter Four) right up through selling it and moving on. After you have these two basics, you get to decide what business maturity means to you.

THINKING DIFFERENTLY ABOUT BUSINESS MATURITY

When I define a mature business this way for my clients, I regularly get the following response: "This makes such great sense, why haven't we heard this before?" I agree. I wish I had been challenged to do this when I was younger.

One of the big reasons we haven't been wired to think this way is because so much of the "entrepreneurial" advice we get is to grow a business so you can sell it. That's supposedly the highest form of business—and sounds sexy, too. The problem is I know of almost no one who wants to pour years of their life into a business just to sell it and walk away.

We didn't invest all those years in our kids to end up with just pictures and stories of the past, and most people who invest years of time, money and energy growing a business don't want to walk away from it, either. Whether consciously or subconsciously (usually the latter), we know that growing a business to sell it sounds like a lot of work just to be put out to pasture or to have to start doing it all over again. So the overwhelming majority of us let talk of that grand, grow-it-to-sell-it scenario go in one ear and out the other.

We don't want to grow a business to sell it, so we assume the alternative is to grow it big enough to throw off some money for us. We hunker down, spend decades focusing on making money, and end up like Samantha—sick of the indispensable trap we've created for ourselves. All we've done by going into business is bought ourselves a job and an immature business requiring looking after for decades.

But somewhere in the middle is an option we never think of, and it's the right one for most of us: stop focusing on making money, build a business that will make money for you while you're on vacation, and then enjoy the business for decades instead of being held hostage by it. Why not build a business someone would love to buy, but then keep it and enjoy it? My wife and I would love it if people wanted to buy our house—that tells us the house is attractive and fun to live in, which is exactly why we have no intention of selling it. We ought to arrive at the same desireable place with our business.

MATURITY BRINGS FREEDOM

Our expectations for our business should be no less than for our kids. If we don't expect our business to grow up, we're still going to be changing its diapers 22 years after we started, unlike the example of Samantha and Cam who rapidly grew beyond that and are now mature, self-sufficient adults.

Remember, Riches equal money, but Wealth equals *the freedom and the ability to choose what to do with your time.* Do you want to be a wealthy person who owns a business that makes money while you are out doing what you want? We'll discover in this book that building a mature business that gives us freedom to enjoy it isn't rocket science—it's not a matter of talent at all, but simply focused intentionality.

Are you in? Will you join me in building a mature business that creates both time and money for you? Does moving from survival through success to significance sound motivating? Let's figure out what it takes to get off the money-making treadmill and build a mature business we can enjoy for decades.

How We Got On the Treadmill and Why We Can't Get Off

Begin with the end in mind.

—STEPHEN COVEY

Most small business owners are not thinking of moving their business from survival through success to significance. Most are too busy spinning their wheels. On average, small-business owners work 52 hours per week (Wells Fargo/Gallup Small Business Index, 08/2005)*. That must have been a poll of the lazy ones. The survey also found that the majority of small business owners work six days a week, and more than one out of five work all seven. One out of seven reported taking zero vacation days in a year, and nearly one out of two said that they still answer work-related phone calls and e-mail while on vacation.

Here's something else even more disturbing to me that was compiled from the 2005 U.S. Census data: It turns out that 3 percent of business owners control 86 percent of U.S. revenue,

---

*Wells Fargo/Gallup Small Business Index, 08/2005
https://www.wellsfargo.com/press/2009/20090803_SBI_Q32009

leaving the other 97 percent of business owners to fight over the remaining 14 percent of revenue.

So both time and money are at a premium. All business owners hope that going into business for themselves will result in making more money and having more free time. The opposite is too often the case. Why are most of us working so hard and not gaining ground on the 3 percent? Is it because we're not as smart or talented as they are? I don't believe so. Most of it is simply that we haven't put much thought into how to take our business to a higher level—to maturity.

> Before we get to how to build a mature business, we have to better understand two things:
>
> 1. How we got where we are, and
> 2. Why we can't get off the treadmill.

These may seem obvious, but as with raising kids, there is a lot of "how" and "why" on the road to maturity. So, we need to first understand how a business develops and matures.

SEVEN STAGES OF A BUSINESS

As it turns out, there are seven stages in the maturity cycle of a business. Why seven? Okay, there might be five or twelve, but I've found seven that seem clearly different enough to call stages of business. Two of my favorite Irishmen, John Heenan and Mort Murphy, got me thinking about this a few years ago when they identified nine stages of business development. Thanks to them for kick-starting this process that has been so helpful to so many business owners.

As I covered in Chapter One, I don't measure the business against itself because that really tells us very little about what our business is doing to provide us with both time and money. So the *Seven Stages of a Business* describes how the business is affecting the owner, the only sensible measure of success for a privately owned business.

Let's look at these Seven Stages and then we'll figure out how they apply to you.

In this chapter, we'll take a good look at the first four stages, because these are the four that teach us how we got on the treadmill. Stages Five through Seven are the ones that get us off the treadmill. We'll walk through them in the next chapter.

Stage One: Concept & Startup

This is the Stage everyone dreams about. We picture bustling streams of customers coming in and out of our shop, the spreadsheet projections are rosy, and the business model is unassailable.

Concept

Concept doesn't deserve its own stage because it's the dreamer's stage, no money is in the game, and no business is being transacted.

In the early parts of Stage One you are developing your business concept. You pour time and ideas into creating the new business in your head, then on paper, then maybe (very rarely) in a written plan. You gather research and bounce ideas off of people you trust, maybe even buy a prototype to show around. Everybody loves the idea and you're off and running.

Early in this stage, the business focus is on dreaming up the best products and services and thinking through how to become the company that everyone loves.

Funding

In Startup, the business, as well your income is supported by funds coming from outside the business, whether from an investor or your retirement fund. For that reason, your lifestyle is probably just what it was before you started, with the source of "income" changing from real income to fake income (living off the investor or the retirement fund).

THE SEVEN STAGES OF A BUSINESS

	STAGE OF BUSINESS	OWNERS LIFESTYLE AND MINDSET	FOCUS
1	**Concept & Start-Up** Owner pours time & time ideas into creating/getting it off the ground *SALES PERSON*	**Income:** From outside the business. **Lifestyle:** Great, but maintained by savings and outside funds. **Emotions:** Euphoria, the business is off the ground. *"What fun!"* **Biz Focus:** Dream, start, setup, sell	SALES
2	**Survival....**is everything; *"We burn a lot of fuel on take-off."* *SALES PERSON*	**Income:** Going backwards or outside the business. **Lifestyle:** What lifestyle? All available time and money consumed by the business. **Emotions:** Scared or tired *"Didn't think it would be this tough"* **Biz Focus:** Urgently driving sales	SALES
3	**Subsistence** Business breaking even, totally dependent on owner. *CRAFT PERSON*	**Income:** Regularly breaking even—the bleeding has stopped. **Lifestyle:** On hold, but breathing easier. Just "the basics." **Emotions:** "I made it! *If I stop the business stops, but that's ok."* **Biz Focus:** Production. "Need to keep clients or I'll be back in survival." Business totally dependent on owner for all functions.	CRAFT
4	**Stability by Hands-On** Sales expanding. Operations are critical. *CRAFT PERSON*	**Income:** Regularly higher than the bills. Vacation and a hot tub! **Lifestyle:** No time! Too busy producing to enjoy the money. **Emotions:** *"I feel like I'm on a treadmill."* Quiet desperation. **Biz Focus:** Keeping up with expansion, fine tuning production. Business dependent on owner for all functions. MOST DANGEROUS STAGE—least likely to risk growing to Stage 5-7	CRAFT
	Owned by the business	**BUSY MAKING MONEY**	

THE BIG MINDSET SHIFT

Business Owner	BUILDING A BUSINESS THAT MAKES MONEY	
		PROCESS
⑤ **Success (Growth)** **by Walking Around** Organization expanding —others producing, and owner supervising by "walking around." *ASSEMBLY PROCESSES*	**Income:** Prosperous—high income. **Lifestyle:** Too busy managing employees to enjoy the money. **Emotions:** "I'm working for the business, instead of the business working for me." "*The business depends on me too much!*" **Biz Focus:** Others doing the day-to-day, but still supervising it all. Go away for four weeks and chaos can still ensue. OFF THE TREADMILL, BUT STILL SUPERVISING EVERYTHING	
		LEADERSHIP
⑥ **Significance** *False Maturity* *Mgt. In Place!* Business is thriving. Owner gives **vision and** **guidance.** *MGT THROUGH OTHERS*	**Income:** Owners independently wealthy. **Lifestyle:** Seemingly (falsely) Ideal—plenty of time to enjoy the money. Doing what they love, both in and outside the business. **Emotions:** Success: **"Others are finally in place. I'm free!"** **Biz Focus:** "If you need me, I'll be on the golf course." 2ND MOST DANGEROUS STAGE—don't "retire" early.	
		MENTORSHIP
⑦ **Succession** *Maturity* *Mgt. in Charge!* Business is thriving. Owner gives it **vision only.** *MGT BY OTHERS*	**Income:** Owners independently wealthy. **Lifestyle:** Ideal—plenty of time to enjoy the money. Doing what they love both in and outside the business. **Emotions:** *Significance, accomplishment.* **Biz Focus:** "If you need me, that's a problem." SUCCESSION? Just pass on the vision torch to the successor.	

Startup

True Startup only comes when you finally commit money and time to getting started. Until then you're barely in any stage of business, because you're just dreaming. Once the time and money commitment is made, the real fun begins.

The operative emotion in Stage One is a sense of euphoria for having pushed your dream to reality: "What fun!" It's a great stage and should be relished, but not for long. Startup isn't something you want to drag out. Get through it as quickly as possible.

Move Quickly

Very few business owners expect their business to support them right out of the gate. More often than not, the expectation to receive income from outside the business gives the owner a false sense of security and a lack of real intentionality to build a business. We assume it's supposed to be this way, and if we look around at other business startups and some of the really awful advice we get, we're told it could be 18-24 months before the business even breaks even. So we take that 18-24 month window and use every bit of it, burning through outside money like there's no tomorrow, and feeling just fine about it because it's supposed to be this way.

A great friend of mine and fellow business advisor in Virginia, Eddie Drescher, told me about one of his clients who had one fitness franchise open and was about to open another. The national franchise had told him it would take 12 months or so to be profitable because that's how long it took them. As this client was about to open his second center, he told Eddie about this timeline. Eddie immediately challenged him, saying, "Who made that rule?" After talking through it at length, they decided to shoot for profitability in the first three months. Instead the location turned a profit in its first month, and stayed close to break even in the following few months. Rather than burning cash for 12-18 months because he was "supposed" to, he intended to do something much better much sooner, and did so.

Speed of Execution

I believe strongly that the number one indicator of success in an early stage business is not how good your product is, or how smart your marketing is, or your uniqueness, or your funding, or any of those traditional ideas of what makes for success. The number one indicator of success in early stage business is simply speed of execution. Think of that successful six figure sales person you know, or that business owner who seems to turn everything they touch to gold. Almost certainly they are people who, when they get an idea, move on it immediately. Most of us spend way too much time thinking, researching, and planning. We would be better off getting a very basic plan in place and acting on it, and perfecting it as we go.

It's the subject of my next book, but for now I can't encourage you enough to just get moving! Stop thinking about starting up, and if you've started up, stop thinking that it's supposed to last until the end of your cash, then magically switch over to funding itself. Get intentional about getting your business through startup as quickly as you can.

Stage Two: Survival

Why should you get moving fast in Stage One...? To avoid as much of Stage Two as possible! Have you ever seen those guys who take snowmobiles out on frozen lakes and see if they can get them going fast enough to hydroplane across a patch of water? If you can, you'll want to hydroplane across Stage Two. In some cases, no matter how intentional you are about starting up, the Survival stage may be unavoidable, but that doesn't mean you shouldn't try to shorten it as much as possible.

The Most Innovative Stage of a Business

Painful as it can be, there are some very significant benefits that come from Stage Two. Most of the great ideas come at this point because Survival is a very strong motivator—we'll do whatever we need to and be as creative as possible to help us get out of this stage.

So many stories exist of businesses that were bleeding badly and on their last legs. They either had to change direction or die, and as a result found business nirvana for themselves. I can't recommend Stage Two because it's tough, but I can tell you that it is a tremendous opportunity for you—don't squander it by focusing on just surviving. We are faced daily with opportunities cleverly disguised as obstacles. Look at Stage Two as an opportunity, not an obstacle, and you can use it to propel your business to success.

Burning Fuel

What nobody bothered to tell you before you started your business or while you were hanging your first sign in Stage One is this:

We burn a lot of fuel on take off.

An aircraft burns a lot more fuel on take-off than at any other time in the flight. Businesses do the same thing. You may not have thought it would be this tough, but the red carpet of success isn't rolled out very often. If you skipped the survival stage, congratulations. That's rare. At some point in every business I've started, I've had to say "I didn't think it would be this tough." I was burning fuel like mad.

I Need Sales!

As you burn through the funds from "outside the business," the need to generate funds by urgently driving sales becomes the sole focus.

Your lifestyle has deteriorated, or in the worst case, you're in denial and living high on the hog from the last few months of available cash in your 401k. All available time is consumed by figuring out how to get the business past Survival.

The euphoria of Stage One is gone. Time is grinding along, sales aren't coming as fast as projected, and expenses are mounting. Over the first six months or so, the operative emotion gradually turns from "What fun!" to "I didn't think it would be this tough." The spreadsheet projections you put together in the Concept phase are not quite working out as they bump up against the real world. And those customers who were supposed to be banging your door down aren't materializing out of thin air like they were supposed to. With outside funds gone, you need money, and to get money you need clients. Sales become everything.

The Trained Seal—Sales Works!

By this point in your business development, your business is teaching you a very bad habit: making money. As you focus on sales, you get clients and money starts to come in. It's working, or so you think.

The subliminal message from the Tyrant that is our business is "Focus on making money. It's the right thing to do." Your business is that little man behind the curtain in the Wizard of Oz, huffing and puffing, steaming and shouting, training you to give yourself to the wrong activities. It's leading you down a very bad path, developing a business habit that is killing your business—making money. Of course, you don't see it this way because paying this month's bills is a critical need.

Unfortunately the next two stages of business development continue to reinforce this upside down view of success. Stages One and Two focus on Sales—Stages Three and Four focus on production, or the "craft." Unfortunately, the change in focus only reinforces the lie.

Stage Three: Subsistence

"Holy Cow! I broke even last month!" The first time this happens you slump in the chair and stare at the wall with a mixture of disbelief, exhaustion, and growing excitement. This business might be viable after all. Then the celebration begins. Pop the champagne, head for the islands, we've got a real business here! The euphoria you had in Stage One but lost in Stage Two is back.

Not so fast.

Stage Three isn't achieved by breaking even for one month. Don't get ahead of yourself. I wouldn't call my business a Stage

Three business until I hovered around break-even for at least three to four months in a row, maybe longer in some businesses.

In Subsistence, the owner is able to pay all their bills, including their personal ones. The joy of it! For the first time in months there is no red in the ledger at the end of the month, either in the business or in the personal checkbook.

Better than Stage Two, but...

But the euphoria doesn't last long. Subsistence looks great having just emerged from the Survival stage. You go from living in a tent in the desert to a rough cabin with holes in the walls, a subsistence garden, outdoor plumbing, and a muddy creek running nearby. It's not the Taj Mahal, but compared to where you just came from, it seems awfully grand—for a while.

Your lifestyle really hasn't improved from Stage Two. It can't really, because Stage Three doesn't have any fudge room. There's no slush fund. You, the business owner, can pay all your bills, but you hope your car doesn't break down, or that a big customer isn't slow paying their bills. Fancy vacations, or even any vacation, may be out of the question. The business is too fragile. It seems that if you even sneeze, you might lose a customer.

So in Stage Three, your lifestyle is still on hold, but at least you're breathing easier. It's all about the basics, but the basics look great because they're finally paid for.

Focus Moves From Sales to Craft

The business focus shifts to production, delivering on the products and services you worked so hard to sell in Stage Two. You're now fully entrenched as the Producer, the artisan, the craftsperson. Unfortunately, the Tyrant that is your business is still teaching you bad habits.

The operative emotion in Stage Three is, "Wow, I made it! If I stop, the business stops, but I have no intention of stopping." Of course you don't. But Subsistence doesn't look good for long. You get tired of the meager garden that looked great when you first saw it, filtering your water from the muddy creek, the wind whistling through the cracks in the cabin walls, and heading for the outhouse in the middle of the night. It was a great upgrade at the time, but very quickly you begin to see all the holes, literally.

The biggest, scariest hole is the inability to relax at all. The focus on Production is absolutely critical because any snafu can result in the loss of a customer you can't afford to lose because you're living on the edge. Stage Two Survival is right behind you, waiting for you to slide back into it.

So you commit to offer the best product or service you can deliver and devote all your time there—you become a fully dedicated professional or craftsperson. Your personal life is clearly on the back burner because, without this manic focus on the business, you won't ever have a personal life again anyway.

Stage Three can be a difficult stage because you wonder if you'll ever get to relax. Days seem longer than weeks and weeks longer than months. Then, something great happens and you finally get the break you've longed for.

Stage Four: Stability (by Hands On)

That big customer you had courted early in Stage Two, the one who ignored you, finally decides to give you a shot. Or the construction you weren't planning in front of your shop finally ends and people start walking past your storefront again. For the first time you have money left over at the end of the month—actual profit. Until this point, the word "profit" meant "anything I can take home to pay my personal bills." For the first time you understand what your accountant has been trying to explain to you, that Income is not Profit. Profit happens after you pay all your bills and after you pay yourself. And you've got some Profit now!

A new question forms in the business. What will you do with the extra $900 this month? Should you take it home as salary and use it as a down-payment on a hot tub, or buy that shiny object you lusted over a few months ago that you think might help business? Or should you just sit on it until next month and see what happens?

A Stage Four business regularly has more revenue coming in than expenses and salaries going out. If it's not regularly profitable, don't kid yourself—it's still in Stage Three. But when it's regularly profitable, the owner's lifestyle has improved dramatically. Hot tubs, vacations, distractions for the kids—it's all coming back into reach.

A Stage Four business can even generate millions in revenue for the owner, but that big profit will never get either the business or the owner to Stage Five. That's because the Tyrant that is your business is still training you to focus on making money. You're intent on keeping up with the growth and making sure production continues at the level it was when you had only two customers and could lavish all your attention on them.

It's a crazy time. And it's made much crazier because you've focused for three plus stages on making money rather than building a business that makes money, which if you remember, is what you ought to be doing.

Your newfound profit distracts you for quite a while from seeing any problem with remaining in Stage Four. You've moved from the rickety cabin to a beautiful house with indoor plumbing and a grocery store on the corner. They'll even deliver. The lifestyle you've created for your family is great. You've joined the American dream. You've got money, friendly neighbors, and a humming business that keeps the whole thing afloat. You can buy a hot tub and go on vacation a couple times a year. But something is missing—too bad you don't get to enjoy it.

What About Me?

Over time you realize that what you imagined when you started the business looks a lot like the lifestyle your spouse and kids are enjoying. But the constant nagging of the business for your attention prevents you from fully enjoying it like you should. The business is dependent on you for way too many functions, and if you do get away, you are greeted by a pile of problems when you get back. Weekends and vacation seem to be times to just recharge so you can head back into the week with some energy. But using your down time to just recuperate is not what you bought into, or so you thought.

Did You Buy a Business or a Job?

What did you buy into when you started or bought this business? Then it dawns on you: You could have bought the hot tub and gotten a few weeks of vacation a year by just staying in corporate America, and without all the sleepless nights wondering if the business was going to survive.

You realize that what you bought into was a job. You're an employee of yourself and the Tyrant that is your business has trained you well with its command to "Go make money." Why don't you see that you're trapped? Why does it take so long after you arrived in Stage Four for you to realize that your family is enjoying their lifestyle without you? Chances are they aren't even enjoying it all that much because you're not there!

There are two simple reasons why most business owners never get out of Stage Four:

1. The business taught you that making money should be your primary focus. In the first two Stages, the Tyranny of the Urgent had you focus on making sales, and in the next two Stages it had you focus on Producing, being the craftsperson, all because you needed to make money to pay the bills and turn a profit.

2. When you got tired of sending your family to the boat on your way to the office, you looked around and saw other "successful" business owners doing the same thing. They are hard workers who spend more time at work than "the other guys." If you want a successful business, you have to spend a lot of time at work. The business owner who seems to have a lot of free time and a light

heart seems to be a rarity, if you even know one. So they must be the exception. You think that what you're experiencing must be normal.

Quiet desperation sets in—"I feel like I'm on a treadmill, and I don't see a way off." The business hasn't taught you how to get off, and other business owners around you don't seem to be any different. Subconsciously, you have become a hostage to your business, with no end in sight. You believe that this is truly all there is.

A Hostage in Your Business—the Effect of the Unknown
Why the analogy to being a hostage?

A prisoner may not control a lot of the present, but even a prisoner controls their future. They know what the rules are while they're in prison, what good behavior will do to shortening the sentence, and most importantly, exactly to the day when they will be free. There is a date to look forward to when things will be different.

Research shows that being a hostage for a very short period of time has a much more damaging effect on someone than being a prisoner for a much longer period of time. Why?

Because of the unknown.

The rules are unclear or always changing and the prospect is endless captivity, never knowing when it might end or worse yet, how it might end. Unfortunately most business owners are hostages to their business, but this does not make it normal, only average. And it messes with your head daily, as you know. When we as business owners focus on making money, we have no idea where we're going, and therefore by default, we can't possibly know what the rules are for getting there.

Stability—The Most Dangerous Stage
Even with the treadmill problem, Stage Four is the most dangerous stage. It's the first stage where you can have riches ranging from minimal to lavish. You've sweated bullets to get

here, and the urge to escape any future risk to get to another stage keeps you here for the rest of your working life. A Stage Four business can throw off a lot of money, but it won't give you much time to enjoy it.

Worse yet, most of us don't realize there are other stages beyond this. You believe that Stage Four is the pinnacle of success—you're profitable, what more do you want? The only thing left to do is see how much more money you can make than the business hostage next door to you. It's truly the most dangerous stage, as evidenced by the fact that almost every business stops here.

Why do you believe you've "made it?" It is because the Tyranny of the Urgent has overwhelmed the Priority of the Important and claimed you as another victim.

There's hope.

The Way Off the Treadmill

You keep thinking about that one business owner you know who seems to have a light heart and quick step, who can get away from work regularly. And when she does she seems to enjoy the time rather than spending it trying to recover from work. You keep dismissing her as an exception—that's exactly what she is, but that doesn't make her a freak. She's actually quite normal, and the overwhelming majority of business owners who have stalled in Stage Four are not normal at all. They are just average. She is normal.

It's not normal to stop at Stage Four—Stability is only average. Almost everybody is doing it, but for one simple reason: They never intended to do anything else. They intended to make money and that is exactly what they are doing. Remember, asking the right question is 90% of the answer. The question to ask is, "How do I build a mature business, and when do I want to be there?" So far you've probably focused on the wrong question: "How do I make money?"

You can escape the Tyranny of your business and become normal too, if you'll just change the question in your head. That's what the next chapter is about.

The Way Off the Business Treadmill

3

Stand in front of a mirror and ask yourself, 'What would I be doing right now if I wasn't afraid?'

Stages One through Four are the only stages most businesses ever experience. Not because it's extremely hard to get to Stage Five or beyond (I think it's much harder to get from Stage Two to Stage Three), but because we simply don't intend to build a mature business that gets to Stage Five and beyond. Ironically, we truly do get what we intend. What intention do we need to get to Stage Five and beyond?

DECIDE TODAY

Dawn Margowski, a great business friend of mine in Denver, taught me the following Chinese saying:

"The best time to plant a tree is 20 years ago. The next best time is today."

Okay, so you got sucked into making money like everybody else and you never thought intentionally about building a business that makes money while you're on vacation. You've been stuck in Stage Four for months (or years!) and just thought it was normal.

No one has challenged you to think it is normal to do something more. That's okay. There is plenty of time to get it right—in fact, getting it right won't take long at all compared to how long you might be bouncing between Stages Two, Three and Four. Plant your tree today.

BASIC BUSINESS MATURITY

The basics of a mature business are these: you no longer have to be the Producer (even if you choose to continue) and the business makes money while you're on vacation.

That's it.

A mature business can be anything from these two simple things all the way to succession and selling the business—it's up to you to describe what a mature business means to you. I would encourage you though to use the above two benefits as the baseline for business maturity. Anything less and you're still on the treadmill.

It's especially important to remember that business maturity really isn't about the business at all; it's about your lifestyle. The only way to really know that your business is mature is if you are living the way you want to as a result of owning it. The size of your business and how much money it makes doesn't matter; the lifestyle you are experiencing is what counts.

MAKING MONEY IS NOT
AN EMPOWERING VISION

To build a business that provides you the lifestyle you want, you need a vision that motivates you. And guess what? Making money is not an empowering vision. I know plenty of people who've tried it including me.

Eddie Drescher has a client who told him, "After $150,000, it didn't make me any happier to be making $500,000." Some people push the numbers up or down, but you get the point—money never makes life more meaningful.

What we do with it can.

I made healthy six-figure incomes for years before I started The Crankset Group. One day a few years ago, while in one of those jobs, Diane, my much better half, came to me and said, "I don't know how you keep going. I can't take this job any more and I'm not even the one doing it." She was responding to the listlessness, the lack of power and meaning that comes from just making money.

She helped me identify that I hadn't made any connection between the money I was making and what I could do with it to build a life of success and significance for myself, let alone for anyone else. It was as if making money was an objective that lived on its own and had no way of influencing what went on in the rest of my life beyond buying shiny objects.

But I knew intuitively that there is a deep connection between my work, the fruit of that labor, and how I could use that work to create a life of success and significance. It was the turning point that led to starting The Crankset Group. I make a great living now, too, but with better reasons than just making dough. I get out of bed easier and with more purpose.

A successful business owner eventually figures this out. Making money is not an empowering vision; neither is a lifestyle being trapped as an employee of yourself. Either way, if you want to be successful you're going to need to figure out how to build a business that makes money while you're on vacation, as well as while you're also trying to make money. The successful business owners do both—remember *dual tracking?*—and they get to Stage Five and beyond.

Stage Five: Success!

As we've seen, in Stages One through Four you simply bought yourself a job. Stage Five is the beginning of a whole new way of doing business where you stop being a hostage to your business and the business starts serving you.

For the first time, you begin to get a glimmer of what it means to own a business that doesn't own you, to go on vacation without returning to a mess, and to have the business make money while you're away. You move out of the Producer role and move others into it and, for the first time, you manage by walking around, not by making the chairs—the product—yourself.

You are off the treadmill, but you are still too necessary and too close to production to completely relax. Stage Five isn't nirvana, but it's a hotel nearby. And it's like breaking free of the earth's orbit compared to Stage Four—you burn a lot less fuel in space. Let's dive deeper into this.

The Big Mindset Shift

I cannot over-emphasize this concept—it is the crux of the whole problem: To get from Stage Four to Stage Five, you have to shift your focus from making money to building a business that makes money. This mindset shift helps you to stop focusing on the Tyranny of the Urgent (making money) and gets you more focused on The Priority of the Important (building a business) while you make money, while you dual track.

The fundamental shift is that the business owner must realize a sustainable business is rarely built on the production of the owner. It can be built on the talent of the owner, or the vision of the owner, but if the owner is the one making the chairs and hasn't been dual tracking, the business won't leave Stage Four. The owner has to learn to resist spending all their time making money to pay this month's bills, and figure out how to get the business to do it for them.

The overwhelming majority of business owners never figure this out. They have a one-track mind for making money to pay this month's bills. "Wasting time" to work on the future, which brings in no money this month, is simply off the table. And that is the biggest reason most businesses never grow up—the owner simply never intends to build a mature business. They just intend to make money.

From Production to Process

As you recall, in Stages One and Two, sales dominated the owner's activity. In Stages Three and Four, the craft, or Production, dominated his time. To move from Stage Four (Stability) to Stage Five (Success), the owner's thinking changes from Production to Process, from being the Craftsperson to instilling in others the ability to produce like the owner did.

In Stage Five, the owner gets the assembly process out of his head onto paper and then teaches others how to do the Production. Employees know what to do, when to do it, and they come to work everyday clear on how they fit into the big picture. This is not an easy thing to pull off, but most businesses drag it out for years when it should only take months.

This is called Process Mapping. Don't fall asleep on me here. I've done this with hundreds of businesses and when they see how simple it is and how significant the impact is on their business, they wonder why it isn't taught in business school.

> In Stage Five, the owner gets the assembly process out of his head onto paper and then teaches others how to do the Production. This is called Process Mapping.

Process Mapping is quite different than putting together job descriptions and unapproachable training manuals. It is an on-the-ground approach to helping everyone know: 1) what they are supposed to do, and, much more importantly, 2) how they fit into the entire process of delivering to your customer.

Process mapping helps every employee understand clearly that they do not have a job, but are part of a process that is much bigger than them. Process Mapping helps every employee understand that they all have customers, whether they are internal or external.

As a result, they stop asking the question, "Did I do my job?" (a very destructive question) and start asking, "Is my customer happy—will they want to work with me again tomorrow?" We'll talk more about the incredible impact of process mapping in chapter eight.

I'm Already There, Aren't I?

Some business owners are going to look at this and say, "I have a Stage Five Success business because I have other people in the production roles." That's not the test. I've seen plenty of Stage Four businesses with others in the production roles. Remember, you need to measure the success of your business against your lifestyle, not against itself.

The test is what happens when you go on vacation, or more importantly, when you get back. Can you go away for weeks at a time without chaos ensuing? If not, you're still a Stage Four business masquerading as a Stage Five. It's stable in the sense of making money, but it's not successful in the sense of creating wealth (freedom) for the owner. Remember, we're not measuring maturity based on what the business looks like, but on what the owner's lifestyle looks like.

In a Stage Five business, the owner has the income that they envisioned when they started this business. Their lifestyle may still be too busy with work, depending on what their Ideal Lifestyle looks like, but they are having meaningful personal time. And while they often still go home tired, there are times when the weekend is no longer the boxer's corner, set aside solely for triage and recovery, before stumbling back into the fray. Many weekends have become a time to enjoy the fruits of their labor with family and friends. And if a Tuesday afternoon sounds good for golf, the owner doesn't have to look in the mirror anymore and ask the boss for time off—the business will do just fine without them that afternoon.

Many business owners are happy to achieve Stage Five and I couldn't blame them for staying there the rest of their working life. It's not a bad gig, but there are some problems with businesses in this stage. Although the income level can be high, and the lifestyle better than average, most Stage Five businesses still spur the nagging thought, "My business depends on me too much." The owner is usually very heavily involved in the day-to-day and is the go-to guy for all issues big and small.

The owner may be off the treadmill, but they have become a glorified supervisor. Nobody else seems to use their brain, at least not one they bring to work. They're all on autopilot and too many things that break require the direct and immediate attention of the owner to fix them.

You're Now a Business Owner

But even with these pitfalls, Stage Five welcomes you as an actual business owner who is no longer owned by your business. It also offers the beginnings of Wealth—*the freedom and the ability to choose what to do with your time.* I couldn't blame a business owner for wanting to stop here, but there's a lot more freedom at the next stage if the owner is interested in going there. Stage Six is where it starts to get really interesting.

Stage Six: Significance (and False Maturity)

In Stage Six, the business is thriving and the owner is now free to invest time in the things that make a business truly great, it can begin to have a real impact in the community and world around it. Charities are benefiting, the employees are involved in the community, and the owner is thinking about both their own legacy and the legacy of the company: "What will I leave behind? What statement will this place make about me?"

> The biggest tactical difference between Stage Five Success and Stage Six Significance is that the owner is no longer supervising production, but has some form of management in place.

This is the fun stuff—this is why we built our business in the first place. We are now back to the passion that brought us into business in the first place. Just about every business owner would love to be in a position to have the time and money (wealth) to think about how to have an impact in the world beyond just selling widgets. Stage Six Significance is that place.

The operative emotion in Stage Six Significance is, "Others are finally in place and managing this. I'm free!" Remember our definition of Wealth: *the freedom and the ability to choose what to do with my time.* We're really experiencing Wealth in spades now. More money is actually resulting in more time. This is the reward for intentionally moving your business from Stage One Startup through to Stage Six Significance, and you should toast your success.

That is why I've got a champagne toast set up for Friday, February 18, 2011, at 8:30am. That is three years, 11 months, two weeks, and 22½ hours from when I started this business. At that point I plan to have a Stage 6 to 7 crossover business. I'll still choose to be involved in some content development and delivery, so it won't be a pure Stage Seven Succession business. I don't want to be out of my business after that, just doing the things in the business I love. And when I get there, a toast to having moved it from Stage One Startup to Stage Seven Succession in under four years is definitely in order.

The biggest tactical difference between Stage Five Success and Stage Six Significance is that the owner is no longer supervising production, but has some form of management in place (even if it's one of the producers) who can watch the shop and function to some degree on the owner's behalf when they are not around. And if you don't have or want employees, then you will need to find other ways for the business to make money when you're not around (we'll cover three of them later in the book). Hiring employees is not the only way to build a mature business.

The Second Most Dangerous Stage

Management in place is the operative phrase in Stage Six, and it's very important that we understand that. *Management in place,* not *management in charge.* Stage Six is a very dangerous stage from the perspective that since we have management in place, we think we can now go directly to the golf course and work on lowering our handicap. Jerry Hodgkin's story might slow you down a bit.

Jerry invested a number of years building a very successful direct mail company. He bootstrapped it through all the Stages, sweated out the hard early years and pulled the business kicking and screaming into Stage Six Significance. Jerry finally had management in place and was enjoying his newfound freedom. He loved vintage race cars and decided he would reward himself by turning his attention fully to racing. He checked in with his business regularly, but became devoted to the cars. Not more than a year after entering Stage Six Significance he had to shut the business down.

Jerry had gotten ahead of himself and learned the hard way that *management in place* isn't nearly as good as *management in charge.*

After a few years of toiling in the business, it will be very tempting to put a warm body in the management seat and head for the nearest fishing hole. Don't do it. All the work you put into your business could too easily come crashing down around you.

At this stage, the owner gives the business two things: vision and guidance. We want to skip the guidance part and head for the hobby. After all, I'm paying this manager good money and I expect competence. But they are not you yet, and you have to turn them into you. A hired gun is one thing, a loyal servant-leader in your business who has the passion for your customers and your employees is quite another. They have to catch this from you being there and instilling it in them.

One of the problems of heading for the golf course too soon is that the manager you left in place (who really isn't *in charge* yet) will report back regularly that things are great. Jerry checked in regularly to make sure things were going well and his manager always provided rosy projections and said great things about the operation. What else would he say? "I'm scared, I don't know what I'm doing, some big customers are mad, and I'm not sure how to solve any of it"? No, your *manager in place* knows you hired them to be competent and they are going to pretend to be as long as they can.

So, your job now is to train the manager(s), instill in them the pride of being *in charge,* and guide them through the day-to-day until the culture of the company becomes a part of them. They'll have a lot to learn—it took years for you, the owner, to figure it all out; so don't expect your manager to get there in the blink of an eye.

Head for the golf course too soon and you might just lose everything you worked for. You'll want to blame the manager when it was really your desire to pull out too fast that caused the crash. Stick in there for a while, make sure you've passed it all along, and you'll have something special—a business that somebody else will want to buy and you'll never want to sell.

Stage Seven: Succession
(Management in Charge)

You've finally made it! You've invested the time to move from *management in place* (Stage Six) to *management in charge,* from giving both vision and guidance to only vision. The manager has the reins and can guide the ship as long as you communicate clearly where you want to go.

The operative emotions in Stage Seven Succession are a growing sense of significance, accomplishment, and satisfaction at having built the dream. Warren Buffet buys Stage Seven Succession businesses and tells the management he doesn't want to hear from them very often, and if he does, that's a problem—that's the extent of your direct management as well.

In Stage Seven, the business owner has multiple options: They can stay on as CEO or President Emeritus, enjoying the fruits of years of labor, continuing to give vision for the future, and choosing how and when they get involved (in other words, *Wealth)*. They can decide to sell the business, pass it along to their children, or use it to start acquiring other businesses.

It's possible that if your business is in Stage Two through Four or even Five as you read this, you're saying to yourself, "Wouldn't that be nice," but without the conviction that this could actually be you. I'll say it again:

I can't think of any reason why you can't get here, except for one—you really don't intend to.

This is not a gifted person's game; it's an intentional person's game. Ask the right question and you will figure out the answer.

The right question is, "How do I build a mature business, and when do I want to get there?" This isn't about building multi-million dollar businesses with dozens of employees. This is about creating the lifestyle that you want for you and your family. You can do that with almost any size business. And you can even do it without employees. More on that later.

A Business You Can Keep or Sell

Building a mature business isn't about eventually selling it (although you can do that, too). It's about building a business that serves you, that creates the lifestyle you want. It's about building a platform for significance that allows you to serve your community and give you the freedom to travel, golf, volunteer, or whatever other burr you have in your saddle that takes time and money. It's about creating freedom and choice.

If selling your mature business gives you more freedom than keeping it, then by all means sell it. I've worked with a lot of business owners who started out saying, "Let's get this profitable so I can sell it and get the heck out." But after they get there, I remind them of this and many times the response is, "Are you crazy? I'm having too much fun!" I understand the desire to sell and get out when things are tough in Stages Two through Four, but it's possible you'll feel differently once you get the business to Stage Five Success or higher.

The Risks and Why They're Worth Taking

By now, you've probably figured out that the difficulty of the Seven Stages of a Business is that moving from one Stage to the next almost always requires risking money or time, usually both. The climb from Stage One Startup to Stage Three Subsistence is one long cliff face with no breaks. You're in Stage Two Survival almost the whole time and you either keep climbing or rappel down and quit.

Having experienced that incredibly arduous climb to Stage Three Subsistence, we would stay there if we could—we've taken enough risks. But unfortunately there just isn't enough appeal to breaking even to keep our attention, so we have a choice to make: quit the business and go get a job or keep at it to see if we can get to a place of stability.

Once we finally get to Stage Four Stability, we now have something to lose. We're making money, in some cases a lot of it, and taking the risks required to get to Stage Five Success seems too daunting. Even though the voice of quiet desperation is whispering, "Is this all there is?" we weigh what we have with possibly losing it and come to the following conclusion: "The pain I know is better then the pain I have yet to experience."

So we stay stuck in Stage Four for thirty years until, at the end, we sell the business for its assets and customer list.

What we haven't realized is that at every new stage the risks are usually smaller and of shorter duration, and if we'll just keep pushing forward, we'll build up our mental muscles for dealing with them.

WHY STAGE FOUR IS MORE RISKY THAN STAGES FIVE THROUGH SEVEN

Stage Four is a mirage. It looks like a business, but as we've seen, it's at best a well-paying job. The owner's focus on making money keeps them cycling between Stages Four, Three, and Two. Some months or years are great, but outside influences create conditions that move the business back into Stage Three, or even Stage Two. Then the owner has to do the long, hard climb back to profitability before the cycle repeats itself.

When I showed the Seven Stages to one business owner at a workshop in Richmond, Virginia, they immediately recognized the cycle and realized their risks were higher hanging out in Stage Four Stability than they would ever be if they intentionally moved to Stage Five Success.

Here's the math: Let's say your business is in Stage Four and does $200,000 a year and you take home $120,000 because you're the main Producer. The economy goes south and you lose half your revenue. Now your business does $100,000 and you take home $60,000—a drastic hit to your income.

Now suppose your business is in Stage Five—others are producing for you, and because of that, you're business is able to do twice as much revenue, or $400,000 a year. But you are still only taking home $120,000 because you have to pay your producers. The economy goes south, you are forced to lay off some your producers, and you have to take over some of that work yourself. The business retreats back to $200,000 and maybe you only take home $110,000. It's a hit to your lifestyle, but it's not going to crater you.

The more you get out of the producer's role and get others into it, the less you will take a personal hit when revenues are down. In bigger companies with dozens of employees, the owner's income isn't affected at all by down-turns. You are not safer by staying stuck in Stage Four Stability—you are safer by creating some space between you and production. If you are the producer, you are at greater risk than if you have others producing for you.

HOW TO DEAL WITH RISKS

Dealing with risk is actually simple—have a very clear idea of where you are going, what it looks like, when you expect to be there, and then make sure that place is motivating enough for you to push through to the finish line.

Do you know what your business will look like at maturity? Do you know when you want to be there? Most of us have never thought about these things, but if you do, it could be the most motivating thing you've ever done. And each stage will seem shorter and less risky because you've got something so compelling in front of you. The Tyranny of the Urgent will lose its shrill voice as you focus on the Priority of the Important.

SOLVING THE PING-PONG BALL PROBLEM: THE BASICS OF BUILDING A MATURE BUSINESS

Imagine trying to keep eleven ping-pong balls under water with only your ten fingers. You're never done because every time you get the last one submerged, another pops to the surface.

Here's the problem (and it's simple): We're so busy trying to control the eleven ping-pong balls with our *own* ten fingers (the Tyranny of the Urgent) that we don't have time to figure out how to hold down hundreds (the Priority of the Important). It never even dawns on us that it is possible to hold down hundreds because we're too focused on the eleven we're fighting with today.

Here's the solution (it's simple too): Be willing to let a few Urgent ping-pong balls get away to build a business that can hold thousands under the water without using *any* of your own fingers.

As we've seen before, the key is dual tracking—simultaneously paying attention to both the Urgent and the Important, using every activity possible to pay your monthly bills and build a business that makes money while you're on vacation.

The Mechanics of Dual Tracking

There are three things that will prevent us from losing focus and being ruled by the Tyranny of the Urgent: One *Big Why* and Two *Bosses*.

The Big Why

Remember that making money is not an empowering vision, and it won't get you out of bed when money is hard to make. But having a powerful over-arching reason to build a business will carry you through the tough times. What reason could be powerful enough to get you through the toughest times?

Lifetime goals.

What are your lifetime goals that you can achieve through your business? Get a clear picture of what you want to do with your life and you'll have a bigger reason to be in business than just making money. You're also likely to make more money and reach business maturity than if you didn't have this Big Why. We'll cover the Big Why in detail in chapter five.

BOSS #1 — A STRATEGIC PLAN

As we've seen, if you don't have people outside yourself helping you get through the stages of business, you're not going to get reach maturity. So let's introduce a couple bosses and get on with it.

The first boss is a strategic plan. This is not a business plan—those are for banks to graze through before giving you a loan, then your plan sits on a shelf. What I mean is a very simple, twelve-month rolling strategic plan by which you manage every strategic and tactical move in your business. Mine is two pages long.

The four simple components of a strategic plan are:

1. A business vision (the Big Why/values),
2. Mission (the big what . . . your marching orders . . . the *result* you give your customers),
3. One-year to three-year strategies (how you make money),
4. Twelve-month measurable objectives (how you measure success at making money) which result in monthly actions you can take to build a business that makes money while you're on vacation.

A strategic plan that runs your business automatically keeps you balanced between making money today and building a business that makes money. We'll talk more about this in chapter six.

BOSS # 2 — OUTSIDE EYES

A strategic plan that runs your business is great, but you also need others outside your business to help you gain and keep clarity and direction. My business is my baby—my perspective is very biased. Others will have a more objective view and be able to see things I never would. Get a peer advisor or better yet, a full peer advisory group and meet once a month. Get others together who support you and your plan. We'll talk more about this in Chapters Nine and Ten.

The Big Why and the Two Bosses keep us moving toward building a business that makes money while we're on vacation.

Use your lifetime goals, strategic plan and outside eyes on your business to encourage you to spend time on the Important. If you allow the Two Bosses to motivate you to build a business that makes money, you're more likely to build a business that makes a lot of it, and more likely to achieve your lifetime goals.

But before we get our Big Why and Two Bosses in place, we've got one more thing to discuss—deciding when your business will be mature. This simple decision could fundamentally change your business and your lifestyle. Put on your seatbelt.

THE SEVEN STAGES ARE ANALOGOUS TO A SEVEN-STAGE EFFORT AT CLIMBING AN IMAGINARY MOUNTAIN

Imagine you and a bunch of friends are starting out to climb a mountain and that most of the early route you've chosen will be cliff faces, and the mountain actually becomes less steep as you climb. In fact, you could drive up. But where's the fun in that? It's a big mountain and will take a few days to climb the crazy route you've chosen. And near the top are great accommodations, a golf course open just a few months a year, and a spa. You've planned your route up the face and you've got all the gear you need. You know there are various ledges and even small meadows where you can take breaks before getting back on the cliff.

When you start the ascent, the initial feeling is one of euphoria over having gotten off the ground. "What fun!" The experience you planned for so long is finally underway. Just like Stage One Startup. Shortly after leaving the ground, the euphoria is gone because you're sweating and grabbing hand and foot holds to keep yourself on the cliff face. The operative emotion changes to "I didn't think it would be this tough." You're in Stage Two Survival.

The first section of cliff face is the longest, and very shortly you are in survival mode. You think regularly of just rappelling down and being done with it. The cliff face seems to go on forever. You can't see that first ledge above you and you wonder if you'll ever get there. You're about to rappel down and give up when you finally see the ledge right above you. You roll up onto the meager little meadow, and it feels like you've just hit the lottery. You all set up your one-person tents and collapse in exhaustion. Stage Three Stability.

By the next morning the meadow looks more like a ditch and you wonder what you ever saw in it. You have a choice.

You can rappel down, or hit the next cliff to the next meadow. The problem is that the first cliff face was so long and the climb up is so fresh in your mind that you find it very hard to get on the next cliff face. Even though you know that every cliff face for the rest of the climb is shorter than the first one and less dangerous, it's hard to start climbing again. But the ditch (Stage Three) is clearly not a place you can live, and even though a couple people with you decided to rappel down, you reluctantly grab your gear and pull yourself onto the cliff face.

The climb is long and hard, but nothing like the first cliff, and when you get to the second meadow you find a surprise. There is running water, bushes full of berries, and a great cabin somebody has built for hikers coming in the easy route up the mountain. Stage Four Stability. You could stay here for days, or even end the trip here and hike out sideways down the fire road. Most of the people who get to this point do just that, which makes it even more appealing— everyone else seems to bail here, as if that was normal and not just average. Nearly everyone who had started the trip bails here.

But the next morning you decide to push on and grab some more cliff face. This one isn't as long and hard as either of the others, and as you get farther up it becomes less and less steep until you're finally walking up hill. Stage Six Significance. Around a couple bends, in the next meadow are the hotel, golf course, and spa. You arrive at the hotel and immediately begin to enjoy the fruits of all your labor, with a great sense of accomplishment and significance. Stage Seven Succession. You're got a great story to tell, and you wonder what ever happened to the rest of the climbers who bailed half way up.

PART II

GET CLARITY

Focusing on the Priority of the Important

3to5Club:
Is There a Business Maturity
Clock Ticking in Your Head?

4

The secret of getting ahead is getting started.

—MARK TWAIN

ecall the two fundamentals of business maturity:

1. The owner isn't the producer.

2. The business makes money while the owner is on vacation. Your business is throwing off both time and money. Beyond these, a mature business can look like a lot of things, depending on the owner's desire for future involvement.

You can decide that you want to be a Stage Six Significance business, like I did, and stay in a management capacity while providing the guiding light to your business. Or you can move to Stage Seven and become the company myth—the founder who walks the halls occasionally, sponsors charity events, and meets with the management to talk about the future and maintaining clarity of vision. Mrs. Fields and Charles Schwab have become myths in their companies. You can be a myth too, if you intend to be.

Again, this isn't about growing a big business and it certainly isn't about growing one just to sell it. It's simply about growing one you can enjoy. If you would enjoy being the company myth, get to Stage Seven Succession. If you want to keep your finger in the pie, Stage Six Significance is a great place from which to run a business for 30 years.

That's the great thing about business maturity. You get to design your own future lifestyle and then use your company to get there. Do you want a big house on a lake? A non-profit you can call your own? A photo montage that shows you climbed the highest 100 mountains? It's all within your reach if you regularly take three simple steps.

THREE LIFE-CHANGING STEPS

I believe the most profound things are the simplest and these three steps confirm that all over again. And the bigger the decision, the more these three things will change you:

1. *Decide something.*
2. *Pick a date.*
3. *Go public.*

Making a decision is a good thing. But more often than not, we didn't really make one, we just claimed we did. So Step One is by itself just a head-game as we pretend to move forward.

When we pick a date for finishing the task or arriving at the objective, we've started some exciting wheels in motion that could lead to success. But even there, we can always change the date—no big deal.

It's when we take the third step of going public that we are changed. When we set a date and invite others to celebrate it with us, or put it in our newsletter and commit to an event, we are now fully in the game. Going public is like burning bridges—there is no going back. It's a tough thing to do sometimes, but the focus and energy that comes from going public with your decision and your date can't be found by any other means.

A guy named Hawthorne studied productivity in the early 20th century and found out that when we measure things our productivity goes up, but when we measure and report the results, our productivity goes up exponentially. You probably believe in this for weekly and monthly sales reports and other short-term measurements yet leave the biggest objective, growing your business to maturity, completely to chance without commitment to a timeline.

THE SECOND MOST IMPORTANT QUESTION IN BUSINESS

As we've seen, the most important question in business is, "What does my business look like at maturity?" The second most important question closely follows the first, "When?" And it's one of the least asked.

Jeanne Samuelson, a friend of mine who owns a corporate training company, told me how she got started. Or actually didn't. She had all the plans, the syllabus, and the locations. She was building a network, too, but couldn't figure out how to actually get clients. Then she went to a conference for HR professionals (her target market) and about 125 HR execs showed up.

The moderator started the day by asking if anyone had any workshops, seminars, or events to announce, and if so, would they like to pass around a sign-up sheet. Jeanne didn't have anything planned at the time, but realizing this was her best shot to reach 125 people in her target market, she took a yellow pad, made up an event title, put a date on it, and passed it around.

One guy signed up. Jeanne was disappointed in three ways:

1. "Oh, no! Only one guy signed up!"
2. Now she was committed to an event that she hadn't planned and wasn't ready to execute.
3. She would likely lose money on the event.

Even though the event was only four weeks away, she worked hard to not be embarrassed and have only one person there and succeeded in attracting eighteen more HR pros. It was a big success. After a few months of going nowhere in her business, she had made a big splash and was on her way. Why?

Because she decided to do something, and more importantly, *she put a date on it.* She couldn't weasel out of the date because others knew about it and were depending on her to follow through. She had gone public.

It is amazing what happens to us when we take those three simple steps: ***we decide to do something, we put a date on it, and we go public with the date.*** Know anyone who has been engaged for years? That's because they intended to get engaged, not married. When a couple actually decides (intends) to get married, they'll put a date on it and both will be changed forever.

"When?" shouldn't be such an unusual question in business, but there's no secret as to why we avoid it. It actually makes us change. We don't like change, even if we'd make more money in less time by changing. So we "make decisions" without commitment in order to avoid actually succeeding.

A decision is not a decision until we put a date on it. Until then, we're just playing office.

So, you've decided to build a mature business—but what is your Business Maturity Date? Until you have one, it's very unlikely your business will ever reach maturity.

3to5Club

To help us all with this three-step process in building a mature business, I started a new "club" that will be owned by everyone involved, most likely by committed, focused business owners in cities across the world. It's called *3to5Club*. Here's how you become a member?

1. **Make a decision** that a) you will stop trying to make money and will become committed to building a

business that makes money, and b) you will define and describe for yourself what a mature business means to you (it has to make money when you're not there for starters).
2. **Pick a date** when it will be mature—not when you will sell it, but when you will fully enjoy it. And pick a time of day, not just a day (more on why later in the chapter).
3. **Go public.** You won't really change permanently until you take this step.

Why the name *3to5Club?* I've become convinced that it is normal for businesses to grow from inception to basic maturity as I've defined it in three to five years. It is normal, but again, it is unfortunately not average.

Investors almost always want their money back in three or less years, and five years is a worst case scenario. There is all sorts of evidence that growing a business to maturity in three to five years is normal. We all know that woman who, by the time she was 35, had grown and sold four businesses and who is now busy growing her fifth. People like her are not uniquely talented, they're just intentional.

In the best and worst of circumstances, you can grow a mature business in two to seven years, so I'm not rabid about three to five, but I do believe that three to five is not a high bar and is doable by every business. And since most business owners who read this are already in business and have a few stages behind them, it could even work out to be a shorter time frame.

You don't have to pick a date in the 3 to 5 range. What you do have to do is pick something a little scary. If you go out 8, 10, 12 years, I believe the bar isn't high enough to create the urgency you need to be intentional every day about growing your business. So, be ambitiously lazy, get done quicker.

DOG-WALKING WITH INTENTIONALITY
I had a woman tell me last year that she wanted to start a dog-walking business. I asked her when she planned to make her first

million and she looked at me as if I had grown another head. She laughed and said, "Um, I'm walking dogs." I then referred her to a big dog-walking company that did millions a year and had gotten there in less than five years.

How did they do it? They simply intended to. The owners had no intention of walking dogs forever and every intention of building a business that made money while they were on vacation. They got what they intended.

YOUR BUSINESS MATURITY DATE AND INTENTIONALITY

Intentionality is everything. But, does that mean you need to have all the details figured out beforehand? Quite the contrary. I'm guessing I'll look back and laugh at some of my own business projections, some of the things I thought would be big that weren't. I'm not concerned about it at this point, because details follow the clarity intentionality brings.

Intentionality means you commit to the very few actions that will get you where you want to go, and *voila!*—clarity and details. If you're not actively doing those few things, you are not intentional, just playing office.

So, to be intentional with your decision to grow your business to maturity, what is the question you have to ask yourself? That's right—"When?" In fact, the single, most important message you should take away in this book is:

Pick a Business Maturity Date.

It's that simple. Some meaningful day and time in the next three to five years when you will no longer be the producer so that the business can make money when you're not there. It will change you forever—from a business hostage to someone heading straight for freedom (Wealth).

Committing to my Business Maturity Date (BMD) took me past the startup fear and right through the stagnant languishing that most businesses resign themselves to in Stage Four. I don't have time to languish in any of the business stages. I'm on a mission and the clock is ticking loudly in my head, saying, "You're done at 10 a.m."

HOW I ARRIVED AT MY BUSINESS MATURITY DATE

On March 6, 2007, I officially started my business with a Business Leader's Insight Lunch workshop and 24 people in attendance. Three years, 11 months, 2 weeks, and 22½ hours from that date, I will have built a business that makes money while I'm on vacation. Until then, I've got a lot of work to do and the clock is ticking relentlessly.

In case you didn't do the math, I intend to have a mature business at 10 a.m. on Friday, February 18, 2011. On that day, I expect to have a mixed Stage Six – Stage Seven business with others running the day-to-day (see Chapters Two and Three on the Seven Stages of a Business). I know how much money it will make on that day and how much I will take home. After that day, I will continue to work on content development and focused delivery.

Why 10 a.m. on that Friday? At 8:30 that morning, I will have a staff meeting and turn over the business to my staff to run, have an early glass of champagne with them, and be out of the office by 10 a.m. to pack my bags. At 6:10 p.m. that Friday evening my wife and I will be on a plane to Auckland, New Zealand, her dream vacation, for three weeks of celebration. We will land in Auckland at 7:25 a.m. Sunday morning. Including airfare, hotels, food, excursions, shopping money and slush fund, the trip will cost $12,380.

By the way, at the writing of this book I don't have staff. That's not at all important to me because I'll figure out how to get there as long as I know where "there" is and when I need to be there. But, to realize this vision, I have to constantly remind myself that 90 percent of the answer is just asking the right question. I believe

I have the right question: "How do I build a mature business by Friday, February 18, 2011, at 10 a.m.?" With the right question always in front of me, I will figure out the details and the steps of the process along the way.

Does reading this change you even a little bit? Imagine what it's done to me, and what it will do to you when you make the same commitment. It will change you forever.

A BUSINESS MATURITY CLOCK TICKING IN YOUR HEAD

Do you know what changed me most? It was when I decided to pick an exact time of day: 10 a.m. Picking the year 2011 wouldn't have changed me; even picking February wouldn't do it. Picking that specific date, February 18, had an impact, but when I picked the time of day, something very interesting happened—a clock started ticking in my head. I had just figured out how to make the Priority of the Important as Urgent as all the tyrannical things in my business: Time was wasting. I had work to do because I'm outta here at 10 a.m.

I wake up many mornings now thinking, "Oh, crap, I'm done at ten. I've only got until ten in the morning. What do I need to do before ten?" A great and healthy sense of Urgency has been added to the Priority of the Important.

I didn't just pick February 18 out of a hat, either. I have quite a few regular monthly commitments that I always have scheduled for the second and third weeks of the month. This gives me flexibility in the first and fourth weeks to carve out up to two weeks (three when it is a five-week month) to do anything from vacation to professional development. Thursday, February 17, is the last monthly commitment I have for that month.

I also figured I could build a mature business in four years, which put me at February 2011. I did the math and looked to see if it was reasonable to get the business to support my lifestyle goal (see Chapter Five) by that time. I felt comfortable that I could actually beat that. So with this combination of factors, February

18, became the perfect day to shoot for. And 10 a.m. allowed me time to have the quick celebration, get home and packed before leaving for the airport.

And I've been going public with this date for a number of years, starting with friends, lunch talks, workshops, my blog, keynote addresses, and in this book. I wouldn't have done that if I wasn't fully committed to getting there. And if I get there a few months earlier or a few months later, I'll only be glad that I worked so hard to make it happen, because without this commitment, I would still be nowhere close to a mature business twenty years from now.

A CRITICAL DECISION—MAKE IT WISELY

I'm torturing you with these details for a very important reason. Don't pick a Business Maturity Date by the seat of your pants. It's much too important. It's more important than any decision you will ever make in business. In fact, it's the most important business objective you'll ever set. I spent a full weekend and then a number of hours in the following weeks with my much better half, Diane, firming up Friday, February 18, 2011 at 10 a.m.

I drew a clear picture of what the business would look like at that time, what my Ideal Lifestyle would be at that time including how much I would make (more on this chapter five), and what the products or services and revenues the business would produce to make this happen.

As you can see, this is not a willy-nilly, knee-jerk decision. If you pay attention to it, it will change your life. If you don't, it will be just another feel good moment as you parent a business that refuses to grow up, a business that is ruled by the Urgent.

HOW TO PAINT YOUR PICTURE
OF BUSINESS MATURITY

Business maturity isn't defined by what the business looks like, but by the lifestyle it provides for you.

Here are five steps you'll need to take to produce a great lifestyle from your business:

1. *Know your Lifetime Goals.* Why are you doing this? To
   what end? Remember, making money is not an
   empowering vision, especially during those periods when
   making it is extremely tough. We'll figure out how to set
   Lifetime Goals in Chapter Six.

2. *Calculate the time and money required to create the Ideal
   Lifestyle* for living out those Lifetime Goals. Do you
   continue to work or do you devote your time to
   something else? What kind of house is best? How much
   travel money will you need? You can torture this step and
   get paralyzed, but we'll deal with it in the next chapter
   and keep you moving.

3. *Decide when* you want to be in that Ideal Lifestyle. Stop
   reading here if you don't want to put a date on that. The
   when you choose for your Ideal Lifestyle will have a
   direct correlation to the *when* you choose for building a
   mature business. They might even be the same day. But
   without a *when* for your Ideal Lifestyle, don't bother with
   getting a *when* for building a mature business—it won't
   happen. We will deal with this in the next chapter as
   well.

4. Once you know the cost of your Ideal Lifestyle, you can
   now project *how much revenue your business will need to
   generate* to allow you to pull the salary you will need to
   support it, and how it will do it so you have the time
   you need to live out that great lifestyle. Your business
   needs to generate both time and money for you, not just
   money.
      An important aside here—it always amazes me that,
   at the beginning of the year, a business owner will pull a
   growth number out of the hat for her business without
   basing it on future objectives. She'll say, "I guess I'll

grow my business by 20 percent this year," as if it's a silly game to be played. This is Important, because if you know what your Ideal Lifestyle costs, and *when* you want to be there, you can divide by the time left to get there and have a very clear picture of how much your business needs to grow this year.

Now the Important has a sense of Urgency it didn't have before.

5. *Develop a very simple plan that shows how your business will generate both the time and the money needed to live your Ideal Lifestyle in support of your Lifetime Goals.* I use a simple, two-page Strategic Plan to run my business on a daily basis. Most of my clients have found it works for them as well. We'll describe it later in the book.

CONNECT THE DOTS

In the coming chapters we'll learn how to discover our Lifetime Goals (we're already doing them!), our Ideal Lifestyle, and how to build a Strategic Plan to use our business to get us to them.

Once you have these business building blocks in place, there is only one thing left to do: Pick your Business Maturity Date and have a great reason for why you picked that date. Make it as meaningful as possible.

It doesn't have to be derived from a tortured business analysis. It can be your birthday, or the 5th anniversary of the day you went into business. But have a good justification for why you picked that year, month, day, and hour. Jan Radin, who owns an emergency medical clinic, picked her deceased father's birthday three years down the road, because her dad was a great business owner and she wanted to honor him by arriving at business maturity on his birthday.

You'll know you have a good enough picture when your excitement level for getting there has gone way up. And remember, the objective of a Business Maturity Date is not to figure out the process of getting there, but simply where "there" is. Find your Mount Doom, figure out the first few steps, and get your ship moving.

WHAT IF I DON'T MAKE IT?

The craziest backwards logic is at play here: "I'm afraid of not making my BMD, so I won't try at all." This is tortured thinking, but unfortunately very common.

I'm not going to give you ten motivational reasons for getting beyond it. I've found in years of working with people that this is one of the favorite places business owners like to hide. "As long as I don't make a decision, put a date on it, and go public, I don't have to worry about failing." Well guess what:

A man still finds his destiny on the path he took to avoid it.

I can tell you with 100 percent certainty that you will fail to get to your Business Maturity Date if you do not set one, go public, and get after it. I've got a much better chance of getting to my Business Maturity Date than not, because I'm working with Intentionality to get there. Don't want to fail? You've already chosen to if you've decided not to try.

FEAR THE PROBABLE, NOT THE POSSIBLE

If my business is not mature on Friday, February 18, 2011 at 10 a.m., have I failed? No, I've had an incredibly rewarding journey that I would have missed if I hadn't tried. And if it takes me an extra six months or year to get there, then I only made it at all because I tried. If I don't try, I'm doomed to live out the Stage Four Stability treadmill nightmare that 95 percent of all businesses have resigned themselves to. That is certain failure, and that is definitely something to fear.

Fear the probable, not the possible. It's possible you won't make your Business Maturity Date, but your failure is much more probable if you don't try.

As Yoda says in the *The Empire Strikes Back*, "Do, or do not. There is no try."

GO PUBLIC

After you've decided to grow a mature business and you've set a Business Maturity Date, don't forget to go as public as you can. Tell everyone. Start something like a *3to5Club* in your area—I'll even give you stuff to help you do it. Put your Business Maturity Date on your wall, in your wallet, on the dashboard of your car, as a screen saver. Find four to five other crazy business owners who will do it with you and meet with them monthly to figure out how to push each other forward.

This is business life and death. Treat it that way.

The next chapters will give you more concrete help to turn your vision into reality.

Dare to be normal, not average. Start a *3to5Club* in your area and be the leader of a revolution from average to normal. Contact us at: Grow@CranksetGroup.com or visit the 3to5Club website at www.3to5Club.com

The Stuff You Can't Ignore If You Want Your Business to Grow Up

Every business should generate time, money and significance for us. Why do we only ask it to make money?

—CHUCK BLAKEMAN

There are four building blocks upon which all privately owned businesses should be founded. They exist whether we pay attention to them or not. Most of us can't take the time to see this because we're stuck on the treadmill, busy trying to make money.

We'll unpack these fully in the next three chapters, but we need to have a context for why the next few chapters are so important if you want to grow a business that makes money while you're on vacation. You ignore the things in this chapter at your own peril because they are out there affecting everything you do in business. These things are all connected to one another in building a business. Nothing in life or business stands apart from anything else—it's all connected. If you don't take control of them, you are going to wonder why it always feels like your business is leading you by the nose.

Let's look at the connection between these four fundamentals and how each one builds on the foundation of the others.

THE PURPOSE OF A BUSINESS

The purpose of a business is to *acquire and retain customers profitably.* If you acquire and don't retain, you're out of business. If you have a small group of long-term customers but can't get anymore, you'll go out of business. If you are really good at both acquiring and retaining, but you don't do it profitably, you're still headed out of business. So we need to do all three: acquire, retain, and be profitable. Everything I can think of in business is wrapped up in these three things. But, as we now know, this is not all there is.

The First Building Block—Lifetime Goals

The purpose of *owning* a business is quite different from the purpose of business itself—it is simply *to create the lifestyle the owner wants for himself, his significant others, and his employees.* It's about lifestyle and significance, not about acquiring or retaining customers. The business takes care of acquiring, retaining, and profit, while we take care of creating a lifestyle out of it that allows us to make an impact in the world around us.

Everyone I know who has started or bought a business had at least the subconscious objective to create a better lifestyle for themselves than what they had when they worked for the Man. Nobody I know goes into business thinking, "Well, this won't allow me to have as much time, money, energy, or freedom as my job did, but I sure am excited about doing it." No, our hope is to make more money in less time than we did before, so we have more money and more time to both enjoy life and leave a more significant impact on the world around us.

Lifetime Goals are at the top of the pyramid because they are personal goals the owner should have that are much bigger than any in his business. Because I have Lifetime Goals, I don't even have business goals anymore—you'll see why in the Lifetime Goals chapter. We should use our business to get us to our lifetime goals, formed by asking questions like,

- "What is my Ideal Lifestyle?"
- "Why do I want to live that way?"
- "What contribution do I want to make to the world and why?"
- "How much will it cost to support that kind of lifestyle and contribution?"

It really makes no sense to build a business until we answer these questions, yet most business owners never once think about why they are building their business, except to say they need to make money, which by now we can see is killing their ability to grow a mature business.

We need to know why we are doing what we are doing. Without clarity on Lifetime Goals, or what I call "The Big Why," we don't have the strongest motivation for building a business. It's no wonder we don't want to get out of bed on the days when we're not making money, because that's all we're focused on—making money. A Big Why would get us out of bed regardless of what any one day holds for us, because we're chasing something much bigger than today's profit or loss. And ironically we would make more money today because of it.

In Chapter Six we'll unpack The Big Why and learn how critical it is to building a business that makes money while you're on vacation.

The Second Building Block—Strategic Plan

I don't like business plans. Nobody looks at them after they get the loan. You should have a simple two-page Strategic Plan instead, by which you run your entire business. We'll learn how to build one in Chapter Seven.

Until you know your Big Why, it doesn't make sense to build a Strategic Plan because you can't answer, "A Strategic Plan for what?" If you don't know what outcome you want the business to produce for you, then how in the world can you move forward? Once you know what your Big Why is and the cost of that Big Why, you can ask a direct business question: "How much money and time does the business need to generate in order to support the lifestyle and world contribution that I want to make?"

Once you know what your personal income needs to be, then it is clear what the business revenue needs to be to produce that kind of income. That's the beginning of a Strategic Plan—how much personal income do I want and when do I want it? We'll unpack the two-page Strategic Plan in Chapter Seven.

By the way, the two biggest hurdles in developing a Strategic Plan are to know your Big Why and picking a Business Maturity Date. If you've read Chapter Two, you're halfway there.

The Third Building Block—Process Mapping

Process Mapping is the tactical outcome of having a Big Why, knowing what it costs to support that lifestyle and coming up with a simple Strategic Plan to get you there. It is the on-the-ground tool ensuring that you work the Strategic Plan and produce the revenue.

I should really come up with a sexier description of this than Process Mapping, but as long as you know it will fundamentally change the way you do business, that should be motivation enough.

Joan Schulte owns half-dozen commercial buildings in the Chicago area. I had told her she would be irked that she paid me to show her something so simple, intuitive, and yet fundamental to her business as Process Mapping. She took one look and said, "Why didn't I do this 15 years ago?" Once you get a feel for it, you'll realize that processes make up a critical building block of a successful business, and that Process Mapping as outlined in this book is the simplest, most practical way to get them working well.

Process Mapping is also the tactical key to getting off the treadmill and finally moving from the revolving rat race of Stage Two Survival, Stage Three Subsistence, and Stage Four Stability to Stage Five Success. In Chapter Eight you'll learn how to do all the Process Mapping you need to move from Stability to Success and beyond.

Nothing else will get you off the treadmill better, faster, or with more clarity and hope than Process Mapping. It's dull, I know, but the surest way to make more money in less time.

The Fourth Building Block—Outside Eyes

Regardless of how much objective knowledge we have about business, we are still subjective about our own work. Everyone has blind spots and everyone needs help to see them. As we sweat over our business to pull it from one stage to the next, we develop an attachment to it that no one else can possibly understand. It's like my kids—I think my kids are the most beautiful kids ever born and I will always love them more than anyone else's. It's just natural. My business is also my baby and I'm a lot more emotional and subjective about it than I might realize.

To balance this, business owners desperately need Outside Eyes on their business. Nothing illustrates this better than an instance in one of my Mastermind groups last year. We were all trying to help Jerry with a specific roadblock that was keeping him from moving from Stage Four to Stage Five. Alex, one of the seven other business owners there, had particularly keen insights and practical actions for Jerry to follow.

Two hours later, when it was his turn to talk about his business, Alex began to outline a roadblock that was almost the same as Jerry's. As Alex took a few minutes to share the issue, I could see everyone looking at each other, smiling and wondering who was going to say it first. Finally, Jerry spoke up and said, "Is it just me or does Alex's issue sound a lot like mine?" Alex stopped, and you could see the wheels turning, and then recognition as the smile came. Everyone had a good laugh and Alex said, "Jerry, do you mind sending me the notes of all those great ideas I gave you. I think I might need them."

It's not about the next guy being smarter, but simply about having others who can objectively speak to our blind spots. Whether it's a business advisor, a peer advisory group like Mastermind, or some other committed outside influence, when we get this kind of help we accelerate our movement from one stage of business to the next in a way we could never do on our own.

THE RUGGED INDIVIDUALIST

For some reason, the American myth of the Rugged Individualist has found a home in business ownership more than anywhere else in our culture. When we get married, we have community; when we move into a house or apartment, we have community; when we get a hobby like golf, we have community; but when we buy a business . . . well, "Good luck with that, you're on your own." From the day we hang our shingle we're supposed to have it all together with no issues. "How's business?" is always followed by "Great!" Meanwhile, we're dying inside wondering if we're driving our business straight toward a cliff.

If there is anything you get out of this book, please get some Outside Eyes on your business that can give you direction and encouragement. There is nothing that will help more. Sure, your baby is beautiful, but wouldn't you want to know if it had chronic medical problems you can't see? Get some Outside Eyes on your business.

TYING IT ALL TOGETHER— HOW WE'LL APPROACH THE PROCESS

We can't give you Outside Eyes on your business by reading this book. You need to go find that building block and get it active in your business. But the process of paying attention to the other three building blocks in the next three chapters is simple:

1. *The Big Why and Ideal Lifestyle Cost*—We need to know our Big Why so we can understand what our Ideal Lifestyle costs.

2. *Business Revenue Objective*—Once we know our Big Why and how much it costs to live that way, we can then ask how much revenue our business needs to generate to throw off the kind of profit and income we need to support our lifestyle.

3. *Strategic Plan*—When we have set our business revenue objective, we can then ask, "How will the business generate that kind of revenue?"

4. *Business Maturity Date*—Once we know how much revenue the business needs to make to support our lifestyle, and how we plan to do that, we then put a date on it to ensure we're committed to building a business that makes money while we're on vacation.

5. *Process Mapping*—We do Process Mapping to work the plan and produce the revenue. If the proof is in the pudding, then Process Mapping is the pudding.

FIRST THINGS FIRST

Before we start unpacking the building blocks of a business in the next three chapters, we need to understand the Seven Elements of a Business. As with the building blocks of a business, these also exist whether we pay attention to them or not. The degree to which we pay attention to all seven will determine whether we will be successful or unsuccessful in building a mature business. We will also use them to build our Strategic Plan and our Process Mapping. So it's critical to get a handle on them.

THE SEVEN ELEMENTS OF A BUSINESS

The Four Building Blocks of a Business—*Lifetime Goals,* a *Strategic Plan, Process Mapping* and *Outside Eyes on Your Business* are heavily influenced by the Seven Elements of a Business. These are used as a checklist to make sure we're covering everything in business that needs to be managed and pushed forward.

All businesses must pay attention to these Elements in order to be successful. Most of us are really good at a few of the seven and unwittingly ignore the other three to four. Small businesses are especially vulnerable to this because the owner relies on her personal strengths and doesn't understand that, until all seven elements are addressed, managed, and contributing to the business, the business will never get out of survival mode. A successful business has the people and systems in place to hum on all seven cylinders.

All great businesses do.

Remember that the purpose of a business is: To acquire and retain customers profitably. All seven Elements help us acquire and retain profitably, and all seven require systems and great relationships to work properly.

Let's take some time to understand each one so we can use them to build a mature business.

ELEMENT ONE—VISION & LEADERSHIP

Stacy Sinjean, a pizza parlor owner, hired an outside advisor (or what I'll refer to as a non-equity partner) because she was smart enough to recognize that she loved the day-to-day and was also really good at developing and managing both systems and people, but she had no idea where all this was supposed to take her. She ended up with four pizza parlors and somebody managing them for her so she could focus on the non-profit work she had started.

All great businesses know where they are going, why they are going there, and when they expect to get there. But, as we've seen, the two most important questions in business—"Why?" and "When?"—are the least asked. Asking these questions is the difference between being a manager of your business and being a leader of your business. Most people just manage, and as a result, never get out of Stage Three Subsistence or Stage Four Stability in order to grow a business to maturity.

I'm not asking you to be some motivational giant here. Just ask "Why?" and "When?" on the big picture level (things that will affect your business for years) and on the small picture level (things that will affect your business in the next few months). If you ask these two questions regularly, you are leading. If not, you are managing. And asking these two questions will help you get a handle on the other six Elements in a way no other question will.

ELEMENT TWO—BUSINESS DEVELOPMENT

Amy Bjorn is a great art director, graphic designer, and project manager who had enjoyed great success for two decades since leaving a large corporation. She came to me one day with a problem—she had no clients left. The seven people who had fed her work for 20 years all retired or moved on within a six month period. Amy had never had to find business on her own.

We worked hard to get her a simple business development strategy and because she was so willing to do the work, she was back on her feet within three months and doing quite well after six. Since then, she has always been diligent to work her business development strategy. She learned the lesson that small businesses cannot afford to separate sales and operations and focus on one at a time.

You need clients. To get clients you need sales, and to get sales you need to understand your message and your market. In order for any of this to work, you need to know that you've got a viable product and that you're continuing to develop it to stay ahead of the changing needs of your customers. Business owners who are focused heavily on production and operations tend to lose sight of this.

Here's a quick tip: Business Development is not a sales process; it is really all about your brand. What is your brand?

1. Your brand is who your customers think you are, not who you think you are.

2. Your brand is what they are buying, which might be entirely different than what you are selling. Have you ever asked your customer, *"What are you buying that I don't even know I'm selling?"* You might have had them at "hello" and are pushing the wrong things on them.

3. Your brand is your ethos, what makes you uniquely you, what the company really believes in and promotes with their actions, not their words.

Ways to Strengthen Your Brand and Develop Business

The stereotypical used car guy focuses quickly on what he can say or do to make the sale. What emotional string can he pull? What weakness can he exploit? Do they hate confrontation? Are they easy to confuse? Do they have big egos? Do they fear losing the car to somebody else? Most importantly, how do they perceive me, the salesperson?

We all want to buy things, but none of us want to be sold anything. I might actually enjoy buying furniture if I didn't have someone in my face as soon as I walk in trying to "answer my questions" (translated: figure out what they can start selling me).

Here's a simple concept: serve, don't sell. Don't ever sell anybody anything—ever. Just serve them where they are in what they need, even if their need has absolutely nothing to do with what you sell. If you were disciplined enough to stop selling your product or service and simply figure out how to serve the people you meet, your sales would increase exponentially.

Why? First, the old sales saw is true—people buy from people (not companies), and they buy the most from people they like the most. Do I get people to like me by being clever or reading body language? No, people like me because I do something that actually helps them move past whatever it is that is standing in their way.

Second, if we serve people in what *they* need, not in what advances our agenda, it builds trust, credibility, and motivation all at once. And the result is, ironically, indebtedness—"You've helped me so much, if there is anything I can ever do for you…" The used car salesman would die to get that kind of loyalty out of a customer. Unfortunately he just wouldn't serve the customer to get there.

You'll read this, but it's not likely that you'll actually apply it. We all "believe" it, but because the benefit is most often delayed (no quick sale), we have trouble actually doing it. You may make fewer quick sales, but you'll make a lot more long-term ones.

Oh, and be prepared for this: "My friend said you took care of him in a way that didn't even relate to your business. That's why I'm here to buy from you."

I dare you to not even bring up your business. Just serve people where they are, not where you want them to be. You'll make more money in less time.

ELEMENT THREE—OPERATIONS & DELIVERY

Okay, you make a great product or provide a very unique service. You're in love with it and so are your customers. It's a wonderful product/service. I get it. Now get over it. Your customers aren't buying it—they're buying things you aren't even selling.

This business Element trips up more owners than any other, except Financial Management and possibly Business Development, because we are so in love with our product or service that we lose touch with what people actually want to buy. We stay focused on production quality because we love our widget and want it to be perfect, but more often than not, people are not buying quality. They are buying consistency. They make the quality decision before they leave the house, then they point their car in the direction of the store with the most consistent level of quality.

I met with one of the top digital communications companies in the U.S. to discuss how to improve performance in their many call centers. They were measuring the standard things—call length, one-call resolution percentage, wait time, abandonment, after-call time, number of transfers, etc. The objective was to get the stats to go down and to get all the call centers to mimic the one with the best stats.

The problem was that every call center director had been given the directive to figure it out locally, under the assumption that giving them ownership of the problem would create a better solution. (This is like telling 12 different manufacturing facilities to produce their computers any way they want—great intentions but not a good outcome). I told them that the **call center with the highest quality of customer service was creating as many problems as the call center with the lowest quality of customer service.** How could that be?

Because their customers aren't buying the *highest quality* product or service, they are buying the most *consistent experience*. We're all out there trying to sell the best made chair, the greatest insurance, the grandest piano, and the slickest software. But our customers aren't buying what we're selling.

Don't believe me?

What percentage of Americans, would you say, think McDonalds sells the *best* hamburger? Probably none. Yet they make billions because everyone knows that every McDonalds window you drive-up to will produce the same hamburger coast-to-coast. It's not the best, but it's the same every time—reliable, consistent, and average. We can count on it and McDonalds can take it to the bank. I've heard that Ray Crock had a motto on the wall in his office that said, "In Pursuit of the Most Efficient Hamburger in the World." Notice it did not say the *best* hamburger. And whether this is true or not, it makes the point. We don't buy quality from McDonalds, we buy consistency.

We don't buy quality from Nordstrom's either. Surprised? While Nordstrom's does sell higher quality goods, we're still buying the "Nordstrom's experience." There are dozens of other retailers selling the same stuff, but we drive right by them to pay more for the same

> ...customers aren't buying the highest quality product or service, they are buying the most consistent experience

quality at Nordstrom's so we can get that legendary experience. We're buying consistency there too, not quality.

A realtor once gave a weekend away to a friend for having referred a high-end house to them. They told another friend who also referred a house to this realtor, and they were given a large gift certificate to a high-end department store. The second friend was disappointed. Even though both gifts cost the realtor the same amount of money, the second person was expecting the same experience as the first—a weekend away. Consistency is so important.

Do you have processes in place that create a consistent experience for every customer every time? If not, stop working on making your product so great and start pouring your energies into creating that consistent customer experience. The guy who makes the best chair does not have the most loyal following. It's the guy who "manufactures" the best, most consistent customer experience who has the most loyal followers.

Go ahead—make a great chair, but it had better be the same great chair every time.

One of the major hurdles for smaller businesses is to get the processes out of the owner's head, get them on paper, and then manage those processes. Voila! Process Mapping. It's one of the best ways to move from a Stage Four Stability business to Stage Five Success or beyond. We'll cover this in Chapter Eight. Don't miss it! It could save your business.

ELEMENT FOUR—FINANCIAL MANAGEMENT

A sausage vendor buys his sausages for $1.00 and sells them for $0.95. But he says he isn't worried because he'll make it up in volume. Hmmm.

Jennie Simms had a rocking event-planning business that pulled in $55,000 per month in average revenue. She came to me for help with strategic planning for the future, but what we discovered she really needed help with was a strategic analysis of her past finances. Turns out she was employing the polish sausage vendor strategy. Her revenue was lower than her costs almost every month, but she was okay with that because, after all, Amazon.com didn't turn a profit for years and most businesses go into debt before they eventually turn a profit.

The fact that her revenues were up by 50 percent from the year before only confirmed to her that she was doing it right. She was out of business three months later, having spent her way into such a hole that none of her creditors had the patience to wait it out any longer.

Financial Management is a critical element of business. Almost no small business owner has a good enough grasp of this. Numbers don't just add up, they tell stories. Numbers is the language of business and very few speak "Numberese." Do you know what story your numbers are telling you? If not, you need to learn. You can't ignore this fourth element.

The best book I know on the subject, written so that business owners can actually understand it, is *Financial Intelligence for Entrepreneurs* (there are different versions) by Berman, Knight, and Case. ***Leading and Lagging Indicators—Your Most Important Numbers.*** Beyond a fundamental understanding of revenue, income, profit, loss, and cash flow, the most important financial management you can do is have leading and lagging indicators of success.

We don't get off the treadmill by selling more stuff. We get off the treadmill by increasing our *yield per hour*—making more money in less time. To do that there are 2-4 numbers we must track religiously: One to two lagging indicators, and one to two leading indicators.

Lagging Indicators of Success

Dave Thomas, the founder of Wendy's Hamburgers, only wanted one number reported to him on a regular basis—number of buns sold. He only needed this one number because he had taken the time to figure out which number was the best indicator of past performance. From that number, he could unpack exactly how much profit per bun the business made, how many hamburgers and chicken sandwiches were sold, the number of Frosty's, etc. It was all rolled up into the number of buns sold.

A number like that is a lagging indicator of success. It looks back at things that have already happened and tells us about past performance.

Leading Indicators of Success

We use lagging indicators of success to build leading indicators of success. Lagging indicators (such as our contacts-to-buying conversation ratio and our buying conversation ratio to closing ratio) tell us exactly what to do to move forward. If I look at my lagging indicators and see that I need to contact ten people to get four buying conversations to retain one new customer (lagging indicators), I can use those numbers to build a leading indicator of success.

Suppose I want four new customers a month—these lagging indicators tell me I need 16 buying conversations a month. To make that happen, I need to contact 40 people during the month. My leading indicator of success then becomes 10 contacts and four coffees per week. My lagging indicators tell me with assurance that if I just do that, I'll be okay.

When I first started one of my businesses, my wife Diane would ask me how next month was looking. My best leading indicator of success was "number of coffees" with business owners. If I had four per week set up in advance, I knew we were going to hit our growth numbers. It was that simple.

This sounds like a sales process, not a financial management process, right? That's one of the big mistakes we make as small business owners—tracking the wrong numbers. Knowing exactly how much business we need to generate to pay the bills and grow is the first function of financial management—what is break-even and how do I get past it? I'm emphasizing the leading and lagging indicators because most accountants will give you the break-even information, but virtually none will help you figure out how to actually manage your finances to successful growth. *True financial management starts with knowing exactly how to generate the numbers needed for success.*

If you have more than three to four numbers you are tracking, you are tracking too many numbers. I have two lagging and one leading indicator and that's enough. Beyond that, with exceptions, you're just playing office.

Your Yield Per Hour

Good financial management also begins with a good understanding of your Ideal Lifestyle (which we will discuss in the next chapter). Most business owners never realize that. They just apply the "random hope" business strategy and "hope to make a lot of money." Here's a better financial management tool for determining your income:

Your lifestyle is driven by how much money your business makes and how much time you have left over when you finish working. It's all about *Yield Per Hour* (YPH). Figure out your Ideal Lifestyle in order to know your required Yield Per Hour.

What is your DESIRED hourly rate (YPH)?

- Annual Income (cost of desired lifestyle)? (A)   ($125,000)
- How many weeks per year do you want to work? (B)   48
- How many hours per week do you want to work? (C)   35

A / (BxC) = *your DESIRED hourly rate—in this case, 1,680 hrs per year or $74.40 per hr*

Once you do this, take a look at your activities and see which ones are below your pay grade. This is part of the Process Mapping chapter and I can tell you you'll be stunned to see how much you're doing that is keeping your YPH down. You will be motivated to eliminate some of your tasks or transfer to others the things they are better at, while you focus on your core strengths.

Pricing Your Products/Services

Pricing is a big part of Financial Management. Here's how not to do it—base your pricing on history, fear, feeling, "my experience," dreams, hunger, client situation/pocket book, convenience, or subjective "analysis."

Here are some tips on proper pricing:

1. *Cost*—This is what it costs you to produce your product or service before you make any profit. If you don't know cost of production for each individual product/service, good luck making money! Get some help with this if necessary because it is vital. Some businesses use a pricing model called cost-plus where you add a margin of profit to the actual cost. This is necessary only in highly commoditized businesses, and even there you should figure out a way to add more value to your products and services so you don't have to play the cost-plus game.

   A note about markup and margin—once you know your cost, you can add a markup. You need to know that markup and margin are very different things. If you mark up your cost of $1.00 by 50 percent, your price is $1.50, but your margin is only 33 percent ($1.00 divided by $1.50). A 50 percent markup sounds impressive until you realize it's a 33 percent margin. Don't confuse the two.

2. *Quality*—Never use only the cost-plus model if you can help it. Find out what the market thinks of your product or service. You might find that they see it as very high-end and that you are under-priced for the market. In some cases, you can simply create a high-end feel for your product by giving it a higher price than others in your industry.

3. *Expertise*—Do people perceive you or your product as an industry leader? If so, you can demand a premium.

4. *Client perception (market demand)*—Convenience, "coolness," market niche and other subtleties can all make your product sell at a higher price.

5. *Scarcity/competition*—Is what you do unique or is the market flooded? That will impact your price.

6. *Hazardous duty pay*—Turn low–profit, high-maintenance clients into high-profit, high-maintenance ones, or fire them. They're not worth crimping your YPH.

7. *How busy are you?*—The 95 percent occupancy rule states that if you are more full than 90 to 95 percent, then raise your prices!

8. *Time/complexity*—Are your customers asking something out of the ordinary? Don't give ordinary pricing! If you want to train your customers to abuse you, ignore this rule.

9. *History*—Are you stuck with past pricing? Use Number One through Number Nine in this list with new clients in order to get out of it. Be courageous—raise prices!

I went through this exercise simply because I want you to see that there are many factors involved in pricing, not just how much time it took you. Almost without exception, the companies I work with set their prices too low. Hike them until you get regular resistance, then you're probably in the ball park.

ELEMENT FIVE—CUSTOMER SATISFACTION

I have done keynote addresses and workshops on this subject and I always survey the audience, asking them, "How many of you have a written operations process of some sort or another?" A majority of hands go up. "How many have a written marketing plan?" Half as many go up. "How many have a written customer satisfaction plan you're using?" If I get five out of 100 hands I'm lucky.

Almost no one has a process for this critical element of a business. Almost every business gets the overwhelming number of future clients from their existing or past ones, yet if you looked at their marketing budgets, the money is going toward impersonal shotgun advertising (TV, Radio, Print), direct marketing (mail, cold calls, email) or, slightly better, Public Relations (events, writing an article, etc.).

There is nothing wrong with advertising but most small companies should invest the majority of their budget in building relationships with existing and past clients until they have a pretty sizable budget to spend on advertising and direct marketing. The return on investment just isn't there for a small business spending a few thousand dollars a year.

Customer Satisfaction is so important that we'll talk about how to develop a process for it later in the book. It is simply far and away the best way to ensure you have a steady stream of potential clients banging on your door.

ELEMENT SIX—EMPLOYEE SATISFACTION

Earlier in my life I got a job in a small corporation that was doing $8 million a year and $32 million five years later when I left. It looked like a rocking place, but it was really a grand oak that had rotted from the inside and was just waiting for a strong wind to knock it down. When I arrived, there were 310 employees, and after only five years I was the 15th most tenured employee in the company; the turnover rate was 63 percent (the HR director liked me—I got the inside scoop). That means that they lost 126 percent of their employees every two years.

I left because the President made the statement in front of me that many very qualified people had jumped ship thinking they were important, but that "we are able to replace them without any problem." There was an arrogance about the place—a feeling of invincibility. Employees were given only the bare necessities to do their jobs and when one was gone, we would just go get another one.

Two years after I left, the company was down to $10 million a year and a mere shell of its former self. And, by the way, customer satisfaction was one of the company's most important tenants. But they had forgotten about the employees.

The moral of this story is that how you treat your employees is how your customers will be treated. I know this sounds simple, but as always, the most profound things usually are. If you are getting customer service complaints, don't look first at your employees, but at how you treat your employees. There's likely something there you can fix that will help them treat your customers better as well. We will spend more time on this later in the book as well.

ELEMENT SEVEN—COMMUNITY, FAMILY, SELF

How does your business benefit the world around you? As I've said before, the biggest reason I can think of to have a Business Maturity Date is so that I can focus on creating a life of significance. As such, this whole book is about getting to at least Stage Six Significance.

A few years ago, when I stopped growing my own businesses and started helping other business owners, I met Jim Drason who owned a residential fire alarm company. It was a nice $20 million a year business, but Jim was bored to death. He told me, "I'm not really sure why I come into work anymore, except that I have nothing else to do. They really don't need me here."

We talked for a while and I found that Jim loved music and played in the town band. He mentioned he had thought of doing something to help kids in the inner city with music since it had been pulled from the district's curriculum. He had mused that it would take $500,000 to do it, but within a of couple hours talking about it, he was at $5 million. He now had a new reason to build a business because he had to grow it to $30 million to throw off the kind of profit he needed to build his foundation.

Jim had realized his business existed not to make money, but to create significance for him, his employees, and the community around him. It was fun to watch him go at it again with passion and renewed energy.

IN SUMMARY—STAY IN YOUR ELEMENT(S)

The key is to know which Elements you are really good at, and how to get others to cover the Elements you don't enjoy. Sometimes early on, we have to cover them all ourselves, but knowing which ones you're great at and which ones you want to off-load puts you in a better position to get off the treadmill faster and get others doing the things that aren't your cup of tea.

GET OUTSIDE EYES ON YOUR BUSINESS

You should have a pretty good idea just looking at the list which Elements your company is paying attention to, but the best way to be sure is to ask others who know your business well and see if they agree. If they don't, listen to them. They view your business objectively; you view it emotionally (it's your baby, why wouldn't you?). Even though they don't know your business like you do, they are likely to have a better handle on what you're doing well or badly than you ever could.

SYSTEMS AND PROCESSES ARE THE KEY

All Seven Elements require processes that allow you to provide a consistent experience for your clients, reliable processes for your employees, and a stable basis from which to grow profitably.

KEEP IT SIMPLE IS STILL THE RULE

If you can't stand in the middle of the room and share your system for each of the Seven Elements in 30 to120 seconds, it's likely you'll never use it. Systems and processes are not three inch binders that sit on desks. They are a remarkably simple set of efficient, time-tested steps that everyone knows and everyone uses every day. For most businesses, your entire systems manual with all Seven Elements shouldn't be more than a few pages long.

Get all Seven Elements of a Business working for you and you'll be on the path back to the passion that brought you into business in the first place. Get all Seven Elements in place and get off the treadmill.

Remember, the Four Building Blocks of a Business and the Seven Elements of Business are things that exist whether you pay attention to them or not. Great business owners watch them all carefully and use them to move their businesses to maturity. In the following chapters we'll unpack all the tools you need to make sure you're using these Building Blocks and Elements to build a Mature Business that makes money while you're on vacation.

The Single Most Important Question in Business

6

If you don't have a plan for your own life, you'll become part of somebody else's plan for theirs.

—MY GOOD FRIEND, JOHN HEENAN, BELFAST, IRELAND

WHAT AN OLD GUY TOLD ME THAT CHANGED MY LIFE

When I was just starting out, a creepy old guy (about my age—mid-50s) told me that life had a built-in problem. He said, "Chuck, you've got to figure this out. While you're young, you've got all the time and all the energy to enjoy life, but no money. When you get to your middle years, you'll have all the money and all the energy, but no time. And when you're retired, you'll have all the money and all the time, but no energy."

He then went on to say something very profound:

> The key to the most significant life is to figure out how to have all three at once—you'll make a lot bigger impact in the world around you if you can figure that one out.

Lifetime Goals have been foundational for me in figuring out the time, money, and energy conundrum, and how to use my business to solve it.

THE BIG WHY

As responsible business owners, we invest a lot of time in answering the "What" questions: What will I sell? What should my price be? What kind of marketing should I do?

We find "How" questions intriguing as well: How will I find clients? How will I make ends meet this month?

And we're even okay with "Who" and "Where": Who is my ideal client and where do I locate, advertise, and network?

All of these questions—Who, What, Where and How—can be fun to play around with. They are largely theoretical questions—I can answer ALL of them brilliantly and do absolutely nothing, frozen in my tracks but feeling as if I've made great progress. Problem: We're really just playing office again; merely doing complex (but easy) things that make us feel important and help us impress others and ourselves.

The biggest, most important question in business, the one that helps us solve the time/money/energy conundrum, the one that will determine our success, the most important question in business is:

"Why?"

CLARITY, HOPE AND RISK

"Why" is the most important question in business, from the very smallest decision to the biggest. If you're buying a copier, you should ask "Why". And if you're building a business, "Why" is the ultimate first question that all other questions go to for an answer. "Why" answers the vision question—Why are you doing this? It is all about Stage Five Success, Stage Six Significance, and Stage Seven Succession. People with a clear vision for where they are going ("Why am I doing this?") are most likely to get there. Answering "Why" gives us clarity, clarity gives us hope, and hope mitigates risk and causes us to take action we wouldn't otherwise take.

"Why" is the one question that will give you direction more than any other question. And yet we rarely ask it. Why? Good question.

More often than not, we simply don't ask "Why" because the question seems so fuzzy and unrelated to business. But while it may be a difficult question to answer, you are doomed to the treadmill if you don't try, going back and forth between Stages Two through Four for 30 years before you sell your job to the next guy who wants to own a job.

Since "Why" is fuzzy, it takes work to answer it. More often than not we simply don't want to do that kind of hard work because it doesn't pay us money today. Again, making money is killing our business. "Why" is a Priority of the Important question and I'm too busy dealing with Tyranny of the Urgent questions to do the hard work required to answer it. But I'll say again, we get what we intend, and those who have a good answer for "Why are you doing this?" are much more likely to build a Mature business, and do it in three to five years.

GOING ON VACATION AND THE BIG WHY

Lifetime Goals bring clarity by answering Why at the highest level in our business: It's The Big Why. It's the same clarity we get before we go on vacation, only at a much higher level.

Would you go on vacation without knowing where you were going? How much sense would it be to pack a bunch of bathing suits and unwittingly end up at a ski resort? Or fill the car with golf equipment and end up at a boat dock? Or start packing with no idea when you have to be there. What if it's six months later? What if it was yesterday?

Of course it sounds ludicrous—no one would ever do this. We spend hours, sometimes weeks, planning a two-week vacation. I spent six months learning Spanish before going for just two weeks to Spain. I studied in my car and during work breaks. I harassed my poor kids (they knew Spanish and found my interest annoying). I was very focused on planning for that vacation.

How much time and effort do we take planning for how our business will affect the rest of our lives? Not so much. As absurd as it sounds, for years we throw things in the "car" of our business—skis, bathing suits, hiking boots, tuxedos, mittens, flip-flops—going every imaginable direction and trying everything possible, with no real clear end in mind. No one would ever plan a vacation this way, but we're okay running our business this way?

He who aims at nothing hits it every time.

So if you decide to actually find out The Big Why and answer the real question as to why you're in business, kudos to you. You will join the ranks of the few who have not only planned a vacation, but the rest of their lives, too. And you will be one of the few who have learned how to use their business to get them to their Lifetime Goals.

THREE FUNDAMENTAL PRINCIPLES FOR BUILDING LIFETIME GOALS

There are three very important things we need to clarify before starting to build our Lifetime Goals.

- *Principle Number One—**Making money is not an empowering vision.***
  I have never met someone motivated solely by making money. Even in those rare instances when it looked that way, it became obvious the person was in it for the game of business, the challenge of building something, and money was just a measure of how they played the game.

  Athletes who make $10.3 million a year don't hold out for $10.9 million a year because they are motivated by the $600,000. They do it because $10.9 makes them the highest paid at their position and "proves" they are the best.

  But, if you think you're motivated by making money, it will be very tough for you to make it through downturns in the business. If you have a Big Why, something that you're using your business to accomplish, you're much more likely to make it through the tough times than the next guy.

- *Principle Number Two—**A goal realized is no longer motivating.***
  When I was a young kid, I got my first transistor radio and took it to the beach. Very cool—playing tunes while catching rays. In junior high, I got a boom box—much better. And in high school, I got a second one with detachable speakers, almost like a real stereo outfit. I continued to upgrade my stereo equipment until one day a few years ago, having done the whole theater and surround sound thing, I found myself looking at speakers that were $8,000 each. The same manufacturer had $125,000 speakers, too. I just hadn't gotten that far yet. Fortunately I lay down and the feeling went away.

  The point is, every time I reached my goal of buying whichever stereo equipment was on my list, I was very quickly thinking about the next one that was bigger and better. As soon as we get to the first goal, we're thinking about the next one. The joy is in the pursuit, not in the acquisition. A goal realized is no longer motivating.

  So I guess we should never have goals? Wrong—just pick ones you can't ever check off as completed. More on that later.

- *Principle Number Three—**We are made to do something significant.***
  I'm not saying we're all made to be on TV, be President, or invent a cure for cancer. That's a pretty warped view of significance. A man can spend his whole life humbly working at his craft and being a joy to the people around him, and you and I will not comprehend the

breadth and depth of significance he has brought to the world around him.

What I am saying is that we are all made to be and do something significant, whatever that means for you. As my Irish friend John Heenan said, "Chuck, God doesn't make junk, and He didn't make you to fail." No, we are made to succeed in bringing significance and meaning to the world whether it's to a small neighborhood world or the global one. And your Lifetime Goals shouldn't be unattainable, just continuous—always providing an ongoing challenge.

If I am made to do something significant, then I need to get a good handle on what that is. I need to take some time to create a narrative for myself that makes my heart sing and gets me out of bed in the morning. I need the will to succeed that comes from having clarity of life purpose.

So, making money is not an empowering vision, a goal realized is no longer motivating, and I am made to do something significant with my life. These three things drive me to find Lifetime Goals, and use my business to achieve help me achieve them. These three principles also debunk an idea that has been around for a very short period in human history—retirement.

RETIREMENT IS A BANKRUPT INDUSTRIAL AGE IDEA

Retirement is a really bad, bankrupt, Industrial-Age idea and we need to deal with it to understand why Lifetime Goals should replace that concept. I believe it evolved with the advent of large centralized businesses. It wasn't a conspiracy; it just seemed like a good idea from their perspective—get the best 30 to 40 years out of me and leave me with the least productive ones. You know the Golden Rule—"Thems that have the gold make the rules."

What so wrong about retirement? Three critical things:

1. Retirement is a goal realized, and we know that once a goal is realized, we discover it's not what we were promised. A study in the British Medical Journal found those "who retired early at 55 and who were still alive at 65 had a significantly higher mortality than those who retired at 65."* Early retirement actually decreased their lifespan. They were no longer motivated; they were out to pasture. Stick a fork in them—they were done.

2. The very concept of retirement teaches us to put off doing something meaningful and substantial with our lives. I heard it hundreds of times growing up from future pasture-geezers still in their 40's, "When I retire, I'm going to...[fill in the blank.]" What a short-circuited way to live—always hoping for a future time when you're actually free to do something with your life.

3. So, I'm really supposed to work until I'm 65 and *then* begin enjoying life? The not-so-subtle message here is that hard work and play don't mix. You are supposed to live two lives—your work life and your meaningful life—and the ideal way to do it is to live your work life first and hope you have time and energy left to live your meaningful life afterward.

---

*[BMJ 2005;331:995 (29 October), doi:10.1136/bmj.38586.448704.E0 (published 21 October 2005) Paper "Age at retirement and long term survival of an industrial population: prospective cohort study" Shan P Tsai, manager, epidemiology1, Judy K Wendt, senior epidemiologist1, Robin P Donnelly, director, health services1, Geert de Jong, senior health adviser2, Farah S Ahmed, epidemiology research associate1]

MAKE YOUR OWN RULES—REPLACE RETIREMENT WITH LIFETIME GOALS

"Thems that have the gold make the rules," right? Here's a slightly different version I work from: "He who makes the rules wins," and I have decided to play by my rules, not theirs.

I'm changing the rules. Retirement is a bad idea. I'm going to pursue Lifetime Goals instead, because I don't have to wait until I'm 65 to begin to live them out. I can start in my 20s and just continue to increase the time, money, and energy I commit directly to living out those Goals until I get to my Ideal Lifestyle.

I'm not saying you should "go to work" until you're 95. Some people will sell their businesses when they are 35 and never return to a traditional job. However, if you don't have Lifetime Goals to replace that work, you will not be happy—we are made to do something significant, and not just for a short period either, but for our entire lives. This is why retirement is such a bad idea. If you choose not work, fine, but put your hand to something that creates significance for both you and the world around you. Live significantly.

Remember, Wealth is ***the freedom and the ability to choose what to do with my time.*** The retirement game says you won't be free until you retire. What a load of hooey. Stop living for a future that never arrives. Don't be "that guy" who, when you're gone, others stand at your casket and say, "Too bad he didn't get to enjoy his retirement."

Lifetime Goals give us something to enjoy and find meaning in today and for the rest of our lives. Life should be meaningful, fulfilling, and satisfying today.

USING TIME, MONEY, AND ENERGY TO CREATE SIGNIFICANCE

The definition of a Lifetime Goal is:

A true Lifetime Goal can never really, fully be completed—there is always something more you can do to make it better, more complete. Any goal that can be checked off as complete is not a Lifetime Goal. Been dreaming about that lake house with the thirteenth tee behind you? That is not a Lifetime Goal—it can be checked

> A Lifetime Goal is a goal which can never be checked off.

off and will no longer be motivating. Get a bigger reason to have that house than just having it. What would you use it for? How could it be used to create success and significance for you and the world around you? Answer that and you've got a great reason to have that house.

The red herring we've been fed is that the accumulation of shiny objects is the same as Lifetime Goals. "My lifetime goal is to have $5 million in the bank, a Mercedes, a 6,000 square-foot house, and a nice boat." No it isn't. Remember the three principles of Lifetime Goals are:

1. Making money is not an empowering vision,
2. A goal realized is no longer motivating, and
3. We are made to do something significant.

If you're initially motivated by shiny objects, you'll be sorely disappointed if you don't have a Big Why for having them. The old bumper sticker from the 80's—"He who dies with the most toys wins"—was wrong. No, **he who lives with the most motivating Lifetime Goals wins.**

YOUR IDEAL LIFESTYLE EXISTS TO SUPPORT YOUR LIFETIME GOALS

I've mentioned both "Lifetime Goals" and your "Ideal Lifestyle." There is a significant and simple difference: Your Ideal Lifestyle exists to support your Lifetime Goals. The time, money, and energy you have amassed (basis of your Ideal Lifestyle), exists simply as a resource for living out your Lifetime Goals.

ROOT AND FRUIT

Some people think it's noble not to have an Ideal Lifestyle—that it might be too materialistic to pursue it. I was one of those for a long time. Then John Heenan said to me, "Chuck, your problem is that you give from your root and not from your fruit. How do you expect to be able to keep giving that way? You'll run out of roots. Build a great root system and you'll be able to give more for a longer period of your life."

WHAT ARE LIFETIME GOALS?

Lifetime Goals are about success and significance, which are also Stages Five and Six of a business. They are value-based activities *that you can never check off.* Every one of them is something you can do the rest of your life without ever finishing. As long as you can draw breath and have some health, you can continue to impact the world around you with these things. They will always be motivating. But there is an even more exciting aspect to Lifetime Goals.

LIFETIME GOALS ARE VALUES-BASED, IDEAL LIFESTYLE IS STUFF-BASED

One woman in her 20s came to our Lifetime Goals workshop convinced that her lifetime goal was to put $5 million in the bank and own a big house in both Denver and Orlando. She walked away excited about quadrupling the size of her business and putting other people in charge so she could live a Stage 7 succession lifestyle and use her company to drive the breast cancer charity that had helped her mom so much. Oh, and it was going to take more than the $5 million she had originally planned on—she had a new stretch goal for a much bigger purpose.

We've been taught to think of goals in terms of hard assets and shiny objects. Get a car; buy a house; save money; own a business. A better way to think of shiny objects is to use them to create success and significance for both you and those around you.

People don't build statues to those who had the most toys, but to those who have had the most impact. If you succeed in formulating a Big Why for running your business, you will have a clear picture of what you should do with it to not just enjoy your life, but to live a meaningful one.

Think of it this way. Your Lifetime Goals are success and significance expressed in values and life beliefs. Your Ideal Lifestyle is the hard assets, the time, money, and energy that support your Lifetime Goals. What values describe your life? That tells you what stuff you need to support those values. We get it backwards. We go for the stuff and then try to find a way to use it to add meaning to our lives. If you go for the meaning first, you can be much more focused on getting the right stuff to support the meaning.

In short, if you have enough time, money and assets (your Ideal Lifestyle), you then have the Wealth (freedom) to live out your Lifetime Goals to the fullest.

Lifetime Goals	Ideal Lifestyle
SUCCESS, SIGNIFICANCE	TIME, MONEY, ENERGY
Value-Based Activities, Goals and Life Principles	The Stuff that exists to support your Lifetime Goals

YOU'RE ALREADY LIVING THEM OUT

- Are you painting, writing, or volunteering in a non-profit right now?

- Do you want to travel the rest of your life? Have you already traveled?

- Do you want to help others get a better quality of life? Are you already doing something along those lines?

- Do you want to be a world-class bird expert? Are you already bird-watching?

All of these are things you can never check off as completed. Lifetime Goals are exciting because we don't have to wait until retirement to live them out. We don't even have to wait until our Ideal Lifestyle to do so.

You're already involved in many if not all of your Lifetime Goals. So the only question remaining is, "When can I focus my full attention on my Lifetime Goals?" To answer that question, we have to ask another, "What is the Ideal Lifestyle for me to get me to my Lifetime Goals?"

If you are presently working two hours a week in your favorite charity and can only give $50 a month, would you want to be able to work in that charity 20 hours a week and give $5,000 per month? If you only travel one to two weeks a year right now, would you want to be able to travel three months of the year?

The Ideal Lifestyle is that specific situation unique to you that will give you Wealth—*the freedom and the ability to choose what to do with my time.* The Ideal Lifestyle sets you up to be able to choose how you are significant in the world around you.

Now that we have a clear understanding of what Lifetime Goals are and what an Ideal Lifestyle is, let's get down to business and do the hard work of defining these things for yourself.

FINDING BERMUDA

First, let's build a common narrative we can use. Here's a great one I heard a few years ago from Art Ratdke, a small business consultant in Virginia.

Suppose you want to sail a boat from Norfolk, Virginia to St. George's, Bermuda. What's the first thing you would do to figure out how to get there? Exactly! Until you know where Bermuda is, you have no clue about where you're going. So, let's say Bermuda represents your Lifetime Goals. What is your "Bermuda?"

Plan Backwards From the Goal

Once you've learned the latitude and longitude for St. George's, Bermuda, what is the next step in planning the trip? Most of us would say we should begin to plot the trip from Norfolk, but we would be wrong. A sailor will always start at the destination and plot the trip backward. Why? Bermuda helps us see why.

The island of Bermuda is 21 miles long and no more than two miles wide at its widest. The island is about 570 miles off the coast of North Carolina and sits at a slant, southwest to northeast. The town of St. George's sits on the very north end of the island. If you were coming directly from Norfolk, it might seem reasonable to just head slightly southeast, straight for the north end of the island. If you did that, you would sink your sailboat.

On the east side of Bermuda, and for many miles to the north of Bermuda, sit a series of reefs that would wreck any ship approaching from the west. And while St. George's harbor is on the west side of the island, the only approach to it is from the southeast. But to get to that point safely, a boat has to sail very far north of Bermuda to clear the reefs, come around the back (east) side of the island, head due south and finally turn northwest into the bay. The best way to find all this out is to plan the trip backwards and pretend you're leaving St. George's to sail to Norfolk.

The same is true for any kind of proper goal setting. You should always start your planning with the end in mind and work your way back to the present. You're much less likely to sail the wrong direction and wreck your business.

Another way this analogy is helpful has to do with how sailors treat the daily objective. Since Bermuda is about 600 miles from Norfolk, and a decent day in a 30 ft. sailboat is 120 miles, a sailor would plan five days to get there and then plot each day backwards from Bermuda to Norfolk. Each one of these daily objectives is called a Waypoint, a term that will serve us very well in building our Lifetime Goals.

So we weigh anchor at Norfolk on the first day and head to our first Waypoint, about 120 miles out. However, the wind turns, the current is unreliable, and one of the sails rips. The boat only makes 100 miles and is 10 miles south of the best course. Has the crew failed? No. The day one Waypoint is just that, a point along the way to help you know how you're doing in pursuit of the ultimate objective. So, the crew has not failed, they just have a decision to make. Do they want to push harder the next day, or get to Bermuda a few hours later?

On the second day, the winds are perfect, the current co-operates and the boat performs flawlessly. The crew blows through the Day 2 Waypoint of 240 miles to finish the day at 260 miles. Is this victory? No. It's just another Waypoint to help them know how they're doing on the way to the real goal. And they have another decision to make—sleep in and relax or push forward and get to Bermuda early.

Waypoints are a great way to see all the other objectives along the way to our Lifetime Goals.

1. They help us treat victory and defeat as the impostors they are. We don't get discouraged and we don't get cocky. We just keep moving because we really haven't done anything until we get to our Ideal Lifestyle in support of our Lifetime Goals.

2. They help us deal with the unbalanced western worldview of goal setting. It is very freeing to realize that we don't measure failure or success by where we are relative to a Waypoint. It's just a point along the way to where we really want to go.

Only Lifetime Goals Count
The sailing analogy works great for me because it helps me put goal setting in perspective. I have no goals for anything other than my Lifetime Goals. Everything else is a Waypoint (Milestone or Objective) along the way. I have no goals for my business, just objectives (Waypoints). I can't fail at my business objectives, because they are only a means to an end. If I plan for the business to grow 20 percent in a year and it only grows 15 percent, I have not failed; I simply have a decision to make. Do I want to hustle

a little harder the next year, or simply arrive at my Bermuda a few months later than I had originally planned?

If I plan that same 20 percent growth the next year and grow 35 percent, have I experienced victory? No. I just have a decision to make—relax the following year or keep the accelerator on and get to my Bermuda earlier.

Stop thinking in terms of short-term goals. Keep your Lifetime Goals in focus and set Waypoints to get you there. Your Waypoints will look just like your old annual "goals," but you will have a whole new relationship with them that will be very freeing and motivating. I can chase my Waypoints with total abandon, knowing they are just check points to tell me how I'm doing along the way to my Ideal Lifestyle.

HOW TO SET LIFETIME GOALS

The best way to set Lifetime Goals is as fast as you can. Take no more than four hours, two to three if you can do it. We do this as a three-and-a-half hour workshop, and only 90 minutes of that is setting your Lifetime Goals.

The reason to race through this process is so that you are forced to only pay attention to the big things. This is not a time to muse over each possibility, but to catch the big ideas and write them down.

It's like when I was a kid I would stare down at the side of the country road on the way from our town to Grandma's town 12 miles away. At 40 to 50 miles an hour, everything was a blur. Some things were obvious—there goes a driveway, the bottom of a mailbox, the bottom of a telephone pole, a big rock, etc. Everything else was a green blur. You didn't notice individual flowers or small rocks; just the big stuff was obvious.

LET'S GET STARTED

A big nod to Mort Murphy in Cork, Ireland for many of the mechanics of this process that we have used for so many years now. As you go through this exercise, do it looking down at the road at 40 miles per hour. Resist the temptation to sit and think through things. As thoughts come into your head, write them down. Don't analyze their viability or relevance; just scratch things down on the fly. We'll come back later and clean it all up.

I encourage the use of a timer on your phone, watch, or computer to keep you moving.

Step 1—Your Values Narrative   3 to 5 Minutes

Every decision we make is values driven, whether consciously made or not. So the best way to find out what's really important to us in the long run is to get a good handle on the values that drive us.

Read through the following list of value words in just three to four minutes—use a timer if you have to. As you read, circle the ones that seem to best reflect who you are, the values you hold most closely. They're all good values, but which ones are uniquely yours?

Then, select the ten that are most important to you. Again, the suggestions on the following page are guides—feel free to add any of your own:

Step 1a—Clarifying Your Values   2 to 3 Minutes

After you finish, go back through and reduce your list of ten to five. Get it down to between three and five if you can.

This is a very important exercise to get you focused on the types of things that will be Lifetime Goals for you and you alone.

Step 2—Stream of Desires and   15 Minutes
Lifetime Goal Thoughts

Using the three to five values you came up with in Step 1, and the list of words, phrases, and ideas below, write down *things you want to be, to do, or to have over the course of your lifetime* on a pad of paper or a blank computer document. This will become a random list of desires to work from.

A few of these will end up being the very few things that describe both your Lifetime Goals and your Ideal Lifestyle. We just don't know which ones yet, so write everything down, and don't analyze anything! Just write.

If you run out of things, look again at your list of values and at the words, phrases, and ideas below to trigger more thoughts. Keep pushing ideas out without thinking about them. If you have more to write down when the 15-minute timer goes off, take another minute or two. If you finish early, fine—move on to the next step.

achievement
accomplishment
advancement
adventure
affections
arts
authority

balance
calm
challenge
challenging problems
change and variety
close relationships
community
competence
competition
conformity
country
creativity
decisiveness
democracy
ecological awareness
economic security
effectiveness
ethical practice
excellence
excitement

expertise
challenge

freedom
flexibility
friendship
growth
having a family
helping others
helping society

harmony
family
friendship
honesty
independence
influencing others
integrity
involvement
intellectual status
uniqueness
comfort
location
loyalty
market position
meaningful work
merit
money
openness
order
personal
development
fast living
financial gain

pleasure
predictability
power
privacy
public service
purity
quality of
participation
risk taking
leading
learning
recognition
religion
reputation
responsibility
respect
security
trust
self-respect
sophistication
stability
status
supervision others
time freedom
truth
wisdom
work under pressure
work with others

work alone
fast-paced work

Words to trigger your potential Lifetime Goals

Family   Work   Community   Causes   Neighbors   Personal

All that I could desire:

—for me
—for others that matter to me
—for causes that matter to me

What I want:

—to be
—to do
—to have

...things, objects, aims, ideals, aspirations, ambitions, hopes, feelings, values, virtues, confident expectations, longings, cravings, desires, condition I want in place, limitations I want removed, legacies I want to leave, possessions I want removed, circumstances I want to be want to own, experiences I want to have had, achievements I want to have achieved, hobbies, toys I want to own, trips I want to take, my personal health, houses/s I want to have, boats, charities, clubs I want to belong to, children's' education, retirement, donations, clothing, cars, relationships I want, whether for myself or for others/and/or causes that matter to me.

What do I want to do before I die?

As you go through this exercise, also note Napolean Hill's *The 12 Riches of Life* and how Financial Security is Number Twelve, not Number One on the list below:

1. Positive Mental Attitude	2. Sound Physical Health	3. Harmonious Relationships
4. Freedom from Fear	5. Hope of Achievement	6. Capacity for Faith
7. Sharing/Giving	8. Labor of Love	9. Constant Learning
10. Self-Discipline	11. Understanding People	12. Financial Security

Step 3—Cleaning Up the Stream of Values List   3 to 5 minutes

Take three to five minutes and look back over your stream of values with one question in mind: Is this a duplicate or repetition of an earlier thought?

Step 4—Obvious Weaker Desires   3 to 5 minutes

This is the first point at which you'll do any analysis of what you've written, and even here, make it very cursory and high level. The car is slowing down a bit here, but resist the temptation to get out and walk to see every little detail. Keep moving!

Once you've got a spring-cleaned list, take three to five minutes and shorten the list by eliminating the obvious weaker desires, those desires that, as you look at them, either make no sense (why did I write that down?), or are clearly not something you need to do, be, or have as part of your Lifetime Goals or Ideal Lifestyle.

Step 5—Identify Stronger Desires   4 to 5 minutes

In this step, label each desire as either,

1. a strong desire,
2. a very strong desire, or
3. a non-negotiable/must-have as part of your Lifetime Goals or Ideal Lifestyle.

Step 6—Must–Haves   4 to 5 minutes

Take another pass and determine which of those from step five you can eliminate. Are there any that you could live without being, doing or having in your lifetime? If so, delete them, as long as it doesn't feel like you're cutting into "live wood." This leaves you with a list of true, strong desires.

Step 7—Sorting   5 to 7 minutes

Group your true, strong desires into the following three categories:

1. Things to Be
2. Things to Do
3. Things to Have

Step 8—Grouping   5 to 7 minutes

Are there any similarities that would allow you to group some of the remaining desires into a single desire? For instance, you might have a "To Be" that says, "be a world class climber," a "To Do" that says, "climb the highest 100 mountains in the world," and a "To Have" that says, "get a passport stamp in each country with high mountains." All three of these are clearly just one desire—mountain climbing. Number them all the same (put a "1" beside each of the three), and write down beside the columns "1-Mountain Climbing."

Do this for the remaining list and see if you can get your list of desires down to three to five things. You don't need to have any kind of balance between To Be's, To Do's, and To Have's. They just need to be desires that get you excited to move forward.

Step 9—Themes/Commonalities   5 to 7 minutes

Look for commonalities, ways that some desires relate well with others. For example, you might have mountain climbing, travel, and being fit. This could be the single desire: "Climb mountains all over the world."

Step 10—Resolve Any Conflicts   1 to 5 minutes

If you have one desire that says you want to live on the beach the rest of your life, and another that says you want to ski the rest of your life, you're going to have to resolve this (though, there are places you can live and do both).

Step 11—Pull the Ideal Lifestyle   2 to 5 minutes
Desires To the Side

Look at your remaining list and ask yourself, "Can this be checked off?" If it is possible to check it off, move it off to the side—these are not truly Lifetime Goals, but more than likely they will be very helpful in describing your Ideal Lifestyle that will support your Lifetime Goals. Don't delete them; just move them off to the side.

Step 12—Start Forming Your Lifetime Goals Statement (Your Bermuda)

From the list of remaining desires that can never be checked off, what do you see that is coming together as a short paragraph or quick list of things? A short list of two to four things that you feel could be Lifetime Goals that would bring significance to your life?

Writing Your Lifetime Goals Statement

Lifetime Goals is about moving yourself and your business from survival through success to significance. Your Lifetime Goals should articulate how you expect your life to be significant and this will overflow into the impact your business will make in the world around you as well. Once you know your Lifetime Goals, you can know clearly how to use your business to get there.

Keep your Lifetime Goals statement as short and memorable as possible. A list of two to four things you want to be, do, or have that can never be checked off as complete is even better. This is not a time to wax eloquent, but to put something on paper that will change your life, get you out of bed each morning, and make you want to build a business that makes money while you're on vacation.

Check your statement against the following questions:

1. *Does my statement list values, experiences, and ways I will create success and significance for myself and the world*

around me (remember, Stage Five is about success and Stage Six is about significance—a Mature Business allows for you to find them both.)

This is not a shiny object or lifestyle statement, but a statement about the core values, contributions, and desires that will get you out of bed every morning no matter what the circumstances are that day.

2. *Does it motivate me strongly?* Is it my Bermuda? If your Lifetime Goals statement doesn't jump off the page at you and make you want to figure out how to get there, keep working on it.

3. *Will it carry me through tough times?* This is really another way of seeing if your Lifetime Goals are motivating, if they will carry you across those days or weeks or months when things are lean.

4. *Do they make you want to take strong action?* Your Lifetime Goals should not be a nice thing sitting on your wall, but something that makes you jump up in the morning with a sense of urgency and clarity for today's work. They should be a strong reminder about the Ideal Lifestyle you're working for.

Remember, things that can be checked off should be part of your Ideal Lifestyle or dropped altogether. Here is a short list of things that people think are Lifetime Goals, but can be checked off:

- Making $10 million. You can check that off. "Being financially independent" might be a Lifetime Goal, but I myself would make it one of the descriptions of my Ideal Lifestyle. But "financially independent" could be a gray area, so make it a Lifetime Goal if that gets you out of bed in the morning. Just remember, making money is not an empowering vision.

- Owning that 6,000 square-foot house on a spit of land at the lake with the 13th hole in my backyard. Again, this can all be checked off and is more likely part of the Ideal Lifestyle you would have for supporting a Lifetime Goal of "being outdoors golfing and fishing as much as possible."

- Playing the top 50 golf courses in the world. Great Waypoint, but not a Lifetime Goal. When you're done, you'll be asking yourself, what next? Come up with a more sustainable golf goal like "experience the outdoors and health together with friends the rest of my life."

- Leaving $100,000 to my local charity when I'm gone. You can check it off. Instead, you might want something like, "Give $2,000 a month to my local charity as long as I live, then $100,000 after I'm gone. Also, work in the charity as often as I can."

Get Feedback

Run your Lifetime Goals list/statement by others who know you really well and ask them if they think it sounds like you, and if they think those things can ever be checked off. The more you share these with others, the clearer they will become for you.

An Example

Early on my original Lifetime Goals statement was focused on "leaving the world a better place than I found it, leaving 100 people behind when I die who would say that man made a significant impact in my life, and building communities of people who wanted to do the same." Over the years it has morphed into "Live well by doing good."

Sounds kind of mushy, but as it morphed into this statement, the measures of what it means have become even clearer. I could unpack that statement for 15 minutes telling you exactly all the things I need to put my hand to in order to live it out.

Your Lifetime Goals statement will morph, too. Don't torture it, just get it done and begin to live with it, tweaking it as you go.

Making It All Practical—
What Does This Mean For My Daily Life?

If you know what you want out of life, but you don't know the important steps you need to take in your business to get there, then you are shooting in the dark. We want to make sure that every day going forward counts toward getting you to your Bermuda. Remember, we have to figure out how to make The Priority of the Important as urgent as The Tyranny of the Urgent.

Determining Your Ideal Lifestyle

Once you've got a good first pass on your Lifetime Goals statement, you can now begin to figure out the Ideal Lifestyle you would want to live out those Lifetime Goals. The Ideal Lifestyle is the tangible assets that support your values-driven Lifetime Goals; the time, money, energy and property you will use to get you there.

For example, if you want to ski 12 months of the year, your Ideal Lifestyle probably wouldn't include a beach house, but might include a condo in Colorado and another at a ski resort in Australia. If you want to help kids in Kenya, you probably don't need a big house in Montana.

Jayleen Proxmire came into the Lifetime Goals workshop believing that her Ideal Lifestyle was a big house absolutely crammed with antiques. And since we are usually living out most of our Lifetime Goals by our 20s, she was nearly there in her early 50s. When it came time to share her Lifetime Goals, it included "having an ongoing significant impact in the lives of my grand-children for decades to come."

After she shared that, she then told the group, "But the funny thing is I have trouble getting my kids to bring my grandkids to my house." Everyone in the room looked at each other and wondered who would say it first. Someone finally piped up, "It could have something to do with your antiques." She left the workshop with an overhauled view of her Ideal Lifestyle—she was going to sell her house and buy one on a lake to create an environment where her kids would feel comfortable bringing their kids to Nana's house. And she was going to have one room she could lock for her antiques.

Things To Consider In Building Your Ideal Lifestyle:

1. *Time*—How will I use my time? What will I be doing and how much time will it take?

2. *Geography*—Where in the world would you live in your Ideal Lifestyle? Split time in two places? Live in a Winnebago and tour the U.S.?

3. *Money/things needed*—What large-expense, material goods and travel will you need? Take your best guess at today's prices plus five percent a year: house(s), car(s), boat(s), plane(s), condo, RV, trips (cost per year x 20 years), non-profit/charity support, etc.

Don't Build a Watch!

The cost of your Ideal Lifestyle will unfold more clearly over the first six months to a year of having Lifetime Goals in place. Resist the urge to belabor this for weeks. If you're highly detail-oriented, you'll want to do just that. Fine, but save it for later and trust your intuition—it's much better than you might think. Simply get an estimate for now—it will most likely be very much in the ball park of what you actually need.

Adding Up the Cost

Add up the big ticket items you will need in your Ideal Lifestyle to support your Lifetime Goals.

- *Significance budget*—If you have a favorite non-profit or want to build one, how much will that cost in both cash and ongoing cost? How much will you need if you want to paint, write, compose, or build furniture or houses for others?

- *Experience budget*—What kind of education, travel, theater, golf, hobbies, and other experiences do you want to have as an ongoing part of your Ideal Lifestyle? What is both the cash amount and ongoing cost of this?

- *Stuff/living budget*—To support your significance and experience budgets, what kind of shiny objects will you need? How many houses, cars, boats, airplanes, will you need? And, very importantly, where will you need them? Geography and location will have a big impact on the cost of these items—there are big differences between Kansas, Mexico, and Manhattan. You should include your basic living costs in this number as well.

Financing Your Ideal Lifestyle

There are at least four ways to pay for something in the future:

1. *Save for it*—This is the least likely way to get as much money as you need.

2. *Borrow for it*—This is only a good idea if you have the ongoing means to pay it back, which involves either or both of the following.

3. *Create annuity revenue for it*—Unless you started saving when you were 25, this is the best means of paying for your Ideal Lifestyle.

4. *Build a Mature business* that you can enjoy for decades that funds your Ideal Lifestyle.

The first two are more the traditional view of retirement, especially "save for it." That's one of the reasons retirement is something that happens well into your 60s, because it is very difficult for anyone to save their way to an Ideal Lifestyle. It's actually much easier to build a business or create annuity revenue to do it than it is to save enough money. I believe the best way to get there is a combination of annuity revenue and a Mature business.

Annuity Revenue

There are a number of ways to create annuity revenue. Remember that I said there is no such thing as "passive income"—strike that phrase from your vocabulary. We have to watch, control, and manage our money all the time. As soon as we start thinking things will happen passively, we are in big trouble.

Here are some examples of annuity income:

- *Real estate investment*—If you do it right and create positive cash flow, you can create a good base of annuity income through real estate investing. If you can find trustworthy people, you can invest without knowing real estate (know the people you are working with!), and do much better than in the stock market.

- *Stock market investments*—The problem with this is that it is a form of savings, and savings is generally not a great way to fund your future unless you start very early, because it takes a lot of time for the money to compound. But if you have Midas' touch, you might be able to accelerate the process.

- *Some careers*—If you are a financial planner, insurance agent, or similar business that pays ongoing annuity income for clients, you can eventually build a large book of business that will still need your attention, but not as much as when you were building it.

- *Investing in other people's success*—This is a form of gambling, but it can pay off quite well if they or their companies make it big.

- *Own your own company*—This is the best way I know to create a lot of income fast. I believe that a business can be built from inception to maturity in three to five years, and I've seen many do it, I firmly believe that someone with no savings could be in a position five years later where their company was providing the same income for them that a few million dollars in the bank would have thrown off in interest income.

Building a Mature Business to Fund Your Ideal Lifestyle

One of my clients was just turning the corner and at the age of 45 wanted to start saving $50,000 per year toward his Ideal Lifestyle, which he intended to arrive at by the time he was 50. The problem was that there was no way that $50,000 per year of savings was ever going to get him there in five years. So we looked at what re-investing $50,000 per year in his business would do for him, and saw that it was very likely the growth of his business that would bring in a few million dollars in return for that investment.

Owning your own company is the best way to get there fast and setting a Business Maturity Date is the best way to ensure you are serious about the game you are playing.

Cash vs. Annuity and/or Business Income

Let's look at some specific examples to see how much easier it will be to get to your Ideal Lifestyle using a combination of annuity revenue and ongoing business revenue from your mature business. I've made two assumptions in order to craft these examples:

1. $110,000 in ongoing personal income
2. $500,000 in cash needed to buy material things (boat, travel trailer, condo, etc.) to support your Ideal Lifestyle

Scenario One

Create $55,000 in annuity income (real estate, other investments) and sell the business for $1.1 million. In this scenario, you still need $557,000 in cash savings beyond what is needed to throw off $55,000 in annuity income, which could be millions or a significant investment in real estate or other investments.

Scenario Two

Create $88,000 in annuity income and sell the business for only $500,000. In this scenario you only need to sell your business for $440,000 and only need $202,000 more in cash savings to fund your Ideal Lifestyle. If you create more annuity revenue your cash requirements go down significantly.

Scenario Three

Just keep the business, get it to Stage Six or Seven and enjoy it while it funds your Ideal Lifestyle. Your income would need to be higher ($240,000 would approximately cover mortgage and loan costs to fund the same things as your savings, but your savings requirements are much lower to nonexistent.

Most Ideal Lifestyle's will be funded by a mixture of savings, annuity revenue, loans and owning or selling your business. The following Table details your options:

	SCENARIO **1**	SCENARIO **2**	SCENARIO **3**
	Sell business	Sell business	Keep business
Freedom income (wealth)	$110,000	$110,000	$240,000
Cash for Income at 5%	$2,200,000	$2,200,000	0
Cash for Toys	$500,000	$500,000	0
Total Cash Needed If No Annuity Income	$2,832,000	$2,832,000	0
Annuity Income (or Business Income)	$55,000	$88,000	$240,000
Cash from Sale of Business	$1,100,000	$440,000	0
Long Term Savings Needed at 6%	$557,000	$202,000	0

Robbing Peter to Pay Paul

If you can achieve higher annuity income, you can reduce the amount of cash you'll need. You can borrow more because you are able to support higher payments. Or you can delay the start of your Ideal Lifestyle, save more, and this would require less annual income from your annuity sources because your loan payments would be smaller.

There isn't a best way. You need to do what is most comfortable for you. I know people who have paid cash for their houses and others who put down the minimum. I put as little as I can into a house because I want to use my cash reserves to buy other assets, but that is just me. On the other hand, I always pay cash for used cars because I see them as a simple depreciating liability (not a depreciating asset). Others will buy only new and wait until they find a car dealer running a low-interest loan program.

However you choose to do it, the quickest way to your Ideal Lifestyle is still to build income from your business as an ongoing annuity funding source for your lifestyle.

Clarity, Hope and Risk

I know all this sounds simplistic, but it's not—it's just simple. In Tolkien's *The Lord of the Rings*, Frodo tops a ridge and sees Mt. Doom for the first time. His goal is to throw the ring into the fire within Mt. Doom in order to destroy the evil ravishing Middle Earth. The volcano looks small and distant, and between it and Frodo lies many miles of treacherous mountains, valleys, evil things, and unknown obstacles.

Frodo had no idea how he was going to get through all that to get to Mt. Doom, but it didn't matter because he was crystal clear about the end game. He never knew more than a few steps ahead, but was always very clear about the goal.

If we know where we want to go, we will figure out the journey. Remember that clarity creates the hope needed to take the risks that will lead you to your goal.

What are your Lifetime Goals? What Ideal Lifestyle do you need to support them? When will you reach your Business Maturity Date so you can have that Ideal Lifestyle? If you have clarity about where you're going, you will get excited about how to get there.

Summarizing your Lifetime Goals/Ideal Lifestyle

Use the following or something similar to get all your work onto one page. Remember, complexity is not your friend. If you end up with pages of "information," none of it will change your life. Keep this to one page.

I put this on my wall and made a wallet sized version with the commitment page on the back so I can review it all the time. Look at it every day as you get out of bed!

Name: Date:

Your Personal Vision/ Lifetime Goals Summary Page

A Your Lifetime Goal-**(Identifying Your Lifetime Goals):** These are things that you can never check off as completed (i.e. traveling, time with grandchildren, etc)

_____

_____

_____

B Your Ideal Lifestyle (forget retirement!) **(Details of Your Ideal Lifestyle):** These are the things you can check off as completed (bought house, attained desired income, etc.)

_____

_____

_____

B.5 Waypoint 5 Years from now: (time & money milestones on the way to my Ideal Lifestyle) **(Resources Needed for Your Ideal Lifestyle):**

_____

_____

_____

B.4 **Waypoint "4" Years** from now: (from B.5 above)

_____

_____

_____

B.3 **Waypoint "2" Years** from now: (from B.4 above)

_____

_____

_____

B.2 **Waypoint 12 Months** from now: (from B.3 above)

_____

_____

_____

B.1 **This Month's Waypoint:** (next milestone or next obstacle removal on way to my Ideal Lifestyle?): from B.2 above) REMEMBER, YOU ARE WORKING BACKWARDS; THIS IS THE LAST PLANNING STEP, NOT THE FIRST!

_____

_____

_____

Committing to your Lifetime Goals and Ideal Lifestyle: The Most Important Steps

The most important part of this process, as with any, is:

1. *Make a decision*
2. *Put a date on it*
3. *Go public*

You should use the following form or something similar to commit to your Lifetime Goals. Fill it in, hang it on your wall in a frame, shrink it to wallet size, put it by your bed.

1. When (**a specific date**) do you want/need to have your needed resources—your Ideal Lifestyle—to carry out your Lifetime Goals?

2. What is the first thing you need to do this month to begin to get to your Lifetime Goals?

3. List the **Benefits** of getting to your Lifetime Goals and Ideal Lifestyle:

4. List the **Negatives** of not getting to your Lifetime Goals and Ideal Lifestyle:

5. **Focus**—Spend 5 to10 minutes quietly somewhere focusing deeply and narrowly on what you have written. Internalize the benefits and negatives, **commit** privately to your goal and tell yourself it is not negotiable. Nothing, absolutely nothing, will get in your way.

6. **Review** your goal, next waypoint, and benefits/negatives DAILY.

7. **Do the plan**—*Thinking and feeling do not produce action.* **Action produces thinking and feeling.** Ignore how you feel each day, overcome the apathy, and do what you've committed to doing. Get going on the first Waypoint (**Number Two above**).

The Time, Money, and Energy Conundrum—Solved!

I'm so thankful for that old guy who shared the time, money, and energy conundrum with me over 30 years ago. It has motivated me to understand the importance of dumping the idea of retirement and replacing it with Lifetime Goals so I can be significant today, not when I "retire." This means also enjoying life today, not then. Being able to combine time, money, and energy is a powerful elixir for a life of significance.

The Most Important Question in Business

Most people spend more time planning a two week vacation than figuring out what will make their life significant and describing their Lifetime Goals.

As Henry David Thoreau said, "Most men lead lives of quiet desperation." Don't be most men. Know what you're doing and get a reason to really build your business.

Dare to ask, "Why?" It's the most important question a business owner will ever ask himself or herself.

Now that you have your Lifetime Goals, planning what to do with your business to get you there takes on a whole new meaning. The Big Why gives us a reason to build a business we never had before, and the Two Bosses will keep us on track to get there. Ready for Boss Number One? He's really a pretty simple guy.

PART III

GET EQUIPPED

The Key Tools for Growing a Mature Business

A Simple Plan That Runs Your Business

7

Good business leaders create a vision, articulate the vision, passionately own the vision, and relentlessly drive it to completion.

—JACK WELCH

Your business exists to generate for you the two most valuable resources we have: time and money. Too often we think it is just supposed to provide money, but as we've seen, money alone does not create a successful business. If your business doesn't provide you with time as well, it's going to be nearly impossible to create significance for yourself let alone for your employees or the world around your business. Any plan you put together to run your business should ensure that you end up with more time, not just more money.

We experience running out of money but what we really run out of is time. No matter how hard we try, we can't manage time—it marches on. All we can do is manage our priorities and how we use the limited time we have. If we use it to make money we're likely not going to make it past a Stage Four Stability business model. If we use it to create time for ourselves we'll be on the road from survival through success to significance, both personally and in our business. A simple plan that runs your business will help you manage your priorities and help you build a business that generates both time and money for you.

In Chapter Three, we said that a successful business needs three outside influences to keep us from losing focus and being ruled by the Tyranny of the Urgent: One Big Why and Two Bosses. The Motivator is the Big Why, or your Lifetime Goals. The Two Bosses are a Strategic Plan and Outside Eyes on your business. Let's do a quick review before diving into how to construct a Strategic Plan.

THE MOST IMPORTANT QUESTION IN BUSINESS

As we've seen, the most important question in business is, "Why?" It should be asked after every other question (who, what, when, how, and where). It reveals a lot, and when we answer it on the strategic level ("Why am I doing this?") and on the tactical level ("Why are we buying that shiny object?"), it changes the direction of our business.

It is the ultimate leadership question. If you're not asking it regularly, you're not leading.

THE SECOND MOST IMPORTANT QUESTION IN BUSINESS

As we addressed in Chapter Four, the second most important question in business is "When?" We avoid it like the plague because when we attach it to all the other questions (who, what, where, why and how), we lose control of our future. Instead of managing our plans, we are now managed by our Plan, required to take action and move forward, when we'd rather think about it and play office some more.

Our Lifetime Goals give us the Big Why. A Strategic Plan helps us get a grip on the When. Once we get our ideas and plans out of our head and put them on a simple piece of paper, they take on a life of their own. When they're written and not just in our heads, they become much more available to us during those times of subjectivity.

DUAL TRACKING

A Strategic Plan is also the key driver for dual tracking. It doesn't include any day-to-day stuff—it doesn't need to. The Tyranny of the Urgent—those things that we need to do every day to make money now—manages to find and bug us on its own. Therefore all the Urgent things need to go on a traditional checklist.

The purpose of the Strategic Plan is to bring the Important things to the front of the line, to give them the priority they should have—in a sense, to create urgency where none is visible. The Important things, those things that will help us build a business while we're on vacation, are all quite urgent, they just don't come across that way.

It's like needing to keep your will up-to-date at all times—it's urgent, but it never seems to be. The same is true for all the Important things in business. A Strategic Plan helps us Dual Track both the Tyranny of the Urgent and the Priority of the Important so we can build a mature business.

Remember the four building blocks upon which all privately owned businesses are founded.

Lifetime Goals is the first fundamental for building a great business. Once we know personally what we want out of our business, we can then think about how to build it. It's about clarity of direction—only after we know where we're going on vacation can we begin packing the car. Most business owners are packing their businesses with products, clients, employees and infrastructure without a clue as to why or where it's taking them. We've seen how Lifetime Goals starts the process. Building a very simple Strategic Plan to run the business will move it forward.

In this chapter, we will find out how to build a simple two-page Strategic Plan that replaces the outdated notion of business planning, and gives us a tool that is dynamic and ever-adapting. It will run our business on a daily basis and it will give us a very clear

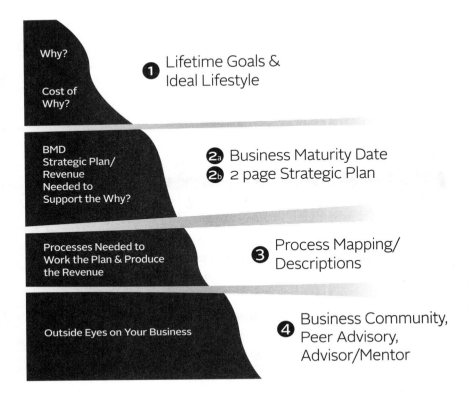

direction, not for three years from now (which we'll never use), but for the next twelve months, three months, and this month.

WHY BUSINESS PLANS DON'T WORK

I lived through a half-dozen tortured business planning sessions in as many years when I worked for large companies. We all went through the motions for a few weeks in January (after the year had already started—I never could figure that one out!), came up with a really impressive 24-page document, put it in a fancy binder, and then shelved and ignored it for twelve months until we did it again. But it made the guys upstairs think we were actually planning for the future.

I advocate that you never do another Business Plan the rest of your life unless you have to get a bank loan, but certainly not to run your business. Nobody uses a Business Plan to actually run their business (at least I've never met someone who does or anyone who knows someone who does). It is woefully rigid and stagnant. It is planned to the penny, and every shiny object needed for the next twelve months is in it. If you had forgotten something necessary for the business, or didn't see it coming, it was too bad. After all, we're not about being effective, we're about following a plan cast in concrete. If we change the plan, we're just showing how incompetent we were when we put it together.

Clearly if the business plan had any value, it would be referred to weekly, updated monthly and heavily revised every quarter. After nine months, it would be revisited and pushed back out to twelve so that we're always actually planning our short term future and never get stuck with a plan that is anything less than nine months out.

If you replace your concept of a business plan with a simple Two-Page Strategic Plan, you'll be much better off.

A TWO-PAGE STRATEGIC PLAN OVERVIEW—BOSS #1

A Strategic Plan is reviewed weekly, revised monthly, updated quarterly and pushed back out to cover twelve months. It is a rolling 12-month plan that runs your business every day. It's your boss. And like any other living creature, it's dynamic, always evolving, never stagnant, or sitting on a shelf. It couldn't stand on a shelf if it wanted to—it's only two pages.

The first page is purely strategic—why you're in business, the impact you want to have on the world around you, and the means by which you make money.

The second page is purely tactical—it outlines what needs to be done in the next 12-months to grow a business that makes money when you're not around. That is then broken down into the next three months, which then reveals what you have to do this month to move forward... Three simple sections— that's it.

Now, for the first time in your business, you will begin to see real monthly progress toward those long-term, fuzzy objectives. Remember from Chapter Six—clarity brings hope, and hope mitigates risk and causes us to take action we wouldn't otherwise take. Our Strategic Plan helps to provide clarity.

The following list is a quick overview of everything you need strategically to build a business that makes money while you're on vacation:

THE STRATEGIC PLAN OVERVIEW
WHAT IS A BUSINESS STRATEGY? IT IS NOT A BUSINESS PLAN.
IT RUNS YOUR BUSINESS DAILY!

VISION *Values*	**WHY?** *Broad, not specific*
BUSINESS MATURITY DATE *Lifetime Goals, end game, end dates*	**WHEN?** *Specific*
MISSION *Results (your customers experience, your marching orders)*	**WHAT?** *Specific, measurable*
STRATEGIES *How we make money*	**HOW?** *How we lead*
12–Month Objectives *Metrics/Measurable Specific/Tactical Timetables Numbers Results!* YOUR MILESTONES: *What are the measurables? When* will each objective be achieved?	**WHAT/WHEN?**
QUARTERLY ACTION PLANS *To carry out the 12-month objectives*	**WHAT/WHEN?**
MONTHLY ACTION PLANS *To carry out the quarterly objectives*	**WHAT/WHEN?**

A NECESSARY HIERARCHY

The Strategic Plan is intentionally built on the above hierarchy. You should always start by developing your Vision Statement. It is the most difficult part of the Strategic Plan (still, your first crack at it shouldn't take more than 15 to20 minutes), but everything falls from it. The Mission Statement is the second most difficult (and not all that hard), but it informs your Strategies.

By the time you work on Strategies, you'll know which direction to take them and they will enable you to decide what your 12-Month Objectives are. Once you've got the 12-Month Objectives, the plan tells you what to do this month to build a business that makes money when you're not around.

> ## USING YOUR STRATEGIC PLAN
> ## TO RUN YOUR BUSINESS EVERY DAY
> **WEEKLY**—Once a week, block out 15-30 minutes to create weekly Action Items.
> **MONTHLY**—Revisit the Monthly Objectives every month to complete the Quarterly.
> **QUARTERLY**—Once per quarter, extend your the plan back out to 12 months.
> **ANNUALLY**—Revisit your whole plan.

A WORD ABOUT BREVITY

Brevity is absolutely key to building a relevant Strategic Plan. We just have to get the right questions and a decent first stab at an answer, because we're going to revise it often to keep pace with the things actually happening in the business.

When you're done with your Strategic Plan (again, the basic plan should never be more than two pages), you should be able to recite your Vision, Mission, Strategies, and 12-month objectives in less than 3 minutes. If you can't, you've got too much detail and you're likely to stop using the Plan as quickly as you created it.

Resist - resist - resist - the urge to include lots of detail. A good Strategic Plan will describe the top line result you need at the end of the month. From that, you can create all the detail that you think you need to accomplish the Objective. Just keep it out of the Strategic Plan itself.

LET'S GET STARTED

A business plan is for bankers. The Strategic Plan is for actually running your business—it's like a compass; don't walk in the woods without it.

There are three guidelines for developing a good Strategic Plan:

1. Get it done in 4-8 hours total—don't get stumped, keep writing, and ask others for input.
2. Keep each line as short as possible.
3. This is not a business plan; it's a strategic plan— dynamic, living, and in-charge!

Weekly	Review the Action Plans every week.
Monthly	Review and update the Objectives every month.
Quarterly	Review and update the Strategies every quarter.
Annually	Review the Mission/Vision annually.

The following pages will lay out the process for developing a simple 2-page Strategic Plan.

Two-Page Strategic Plan
Development Instructions

Use the Strategic Plan template example you'll see later in this chapter or build one to your liking.

STRATEGIC PLAN PAGE ONE
VISION, MISSION, STRATEGIES

SITUATION OVERVIEW

Overview   25 to 50 words   10 to 15 minutes

This is an important warm-up exercise to get you thinking in the right direction. Answer the following questions:

1. What niche are you filling?
2. Who do you serve (target market)?
3. What do you offer (product/service overview)?
4. What makes your business viable? Why do people want to buy from you?

For example, you could say, *"I saw the following opportunity..."; "People need what we have because..."; "Our market is x, we serve by doing x and we have a special focus on x (our niche), or a special focus, offering x service..."*

Here is what I wrote for my Situation Overview: *"We serve small to medium size business owners to help them make more money in less time (YPH), get off the treadmill, and have a mature business that serves their Lifetime Goals. We have two tracks—micro-business owners who need revenue enhancement and small/mid size owners with employees who need to work on all Seven Elements of a Business."*

The Situation Overview isn't for public consumption. If you know what it means—great. It will come in handy as you develop the rest of the Strategic Plan, and it will guide your marketing plan.

YOUR DIFFERENTIATOR

Differentiator   25 to 50 words   10 to 15 minutes
This is a second, very important warm-up exercise. Both this and
the Situation Overview will lay the foundation for everything that
follows—from Vision, Mission, and Strategies to future marketing
and advertising campaigns.

What's the one thing that makes you different than the next
guy selling what you sell? What are you better at that no one else
in your local market can match? You don't have to have a lot of
things that make you special, just one that others don't have. Is
it your personalized service, the uniqueness of your product, your
experience or your location?

Find that one thing that is uniquely you and write it down.
This is your differentiator.

Such as: *We focus only on stairways and do no other interior
trim. We are the experts in our area of town. / We are customer-
focused in an industry that doesn't care…*

Here's my Differentiator:

1. We serve, we do not sell.
2. We live in a world of abundance, not a world of scarcity.
3. The needs of the client govern all decisions regarding them.
4. We are outcome-based, not education-based.
5. We are in the trenches with our clients.
6. We measure growth and progress toward goals.
7. We work from Quantum Business Rules, not Big
   Business Rules.

YOUR VISION STATEMENT

Vision   **1 to 20 words**   **15 to 60 minutes**

Answers the question—WHY?
(Answer is good for long as you're in business.)

Jump Ahead

Before putting together a Vision Statement, read both this section on Vision and the next section on your Mission Statement. Understanding them both will help you understand clearly how they are different. People get Vision and Mission confused all the time and they are a world apart in my Strategic Plan. Reading both first will help you better write each one.

Vision Reflects You and Your Company

The Vision Statement is more for you than for your customers. It is the long term motivation for why you will be in business: your values, your passion, your over-arching and lasting contribution/legacy. It's directly connected to your Big Why and helps you focus on moving your business from success to significance. It doesn't necessarily say exactly what your company does, but it expresses the long-term impact you hope it has in the world around you.

For example, a great vision statement for a company making either scrapbooks or photographic equipment would be "Memories." It's not really about the product, but what the product does.

The shorter your Vision Statement is, the better it is. Mine is, "Live well by doing good." I could be in any number of businesses and live this out, but I know exactly what it means for my business, and it gets me out of bed every morning.

So, write it in terms of **values**. You will measure the success of your Vision by the values it creates, adheres to, promotes, etc.

Here are some things to consider as you get ready to write:

1. What kind of company do you want to be?
2. What do you want to be remembered for?
3. What impact will you have: Locally, Regionally, Nationally, Internationally?
4. What really juices me about my business, the thing behind the product/service that I know will create significance for me, for employees, for customers?
5. What would someone say about your company if they used value words—honest, integrity, enjoy life; live well; serving, hope, complete, etc?

Your Vision Statement should last as long as your business does. Don't worry about getting it perfect—you can clean up the wording next month/quarter. Get started!

"Live Well By Doing Good."

This is my Vision Statement. It means that I expect business owners and their businesses to benefit significantly from contact with The Crankset Group. It means their lives and their businesses will be changed, and they will gladly pay us for that benefit. It also means that I expect to live well by providing these services, and as our business grows we can create more resources for doing good in the lives and businesses of others.

Doing good in those businesses results in revenue that lets us live well, which then provides the resources to do more good, in an ever-expanding circle outward. Having an ever-expanding impact in the lives of others and their businesses is very motivating to me. It gets me out of bed every morning, puts the wind in my sails and has given the tough times real meaning, where making money wouldn't.

What gets you and everyone at your company, out of bed in the morning and running for your car to get to work? What is the story others will tell about you and the impact your business had on their lives beyond what you've sold to them? Are you selling film or building memories? Without a vision, you're just selling film.

YOUR BUSINESS MATURITY DATE

BMD **25 to 50 words** **8 to 36 hours**

Answers the question—WHEN?

See Chapter Four for how to figure your Business Maturity Date (BMD). The BMD is the concrete side of your vision—it's the clear end game. I said the Strategic Plan should only take a few hours to put together, but that's because I'm assuming you've already had an absolutely great time deciding your Business Maturity Date and putting together the picture of what your business looks like on that day, how you will celebrate, etc.

If you haven't, stop here, go back to Chapter Four and get a Business Maturity Date. Until you have a BMD, honestly, the rest of this book is just playing office. It will never have the impact it could have if you actually knew where this is taking you. So we'll assume you've got a BMD to insert here.

My Business Maturity Date statement: *February 18, 10 a.m., 2011. Stage 6-7 business (continue in content development & delivery; others run the business.) $xxxk/yr annuity—$xk per month to non-profit (where "k" means "thousand"). Leave Denver 6:10 p.m.; Arrive Auckland, NZ Sun, 7:25 a.m., 2/20/2011 $2,880 flights; $4,000 for hotels/transportation; $2,200 food; $3,500 entertainment = $12,380*

That trip to New Zealand is a very visual and tangible way of making the Business Maturity Date real to me, and helping me stay committed to it. I encourage you to find any way you can to make your BMD real, tangible, and urgent.

YOUR MISSION STATEMENT

Mission   1 to 40 words   10 to 60 minutes

Answers the question—WHAT?
(Answer is good for long as you're in business.)

Your Mission Statement is entirely different than your Vision Statement. The Vision Statement is value-based, general, maybe even a little mysterious, but certainly focused on motivation. And although you certainly can make it public, it's not intended for the public—they might not even get it.

Your Mission Statement is very much designed to be shared openly and often with your customers, your employees, your community, and anyone else who will lend an ear. It is very specific, not general like the Vision Statement.

The Mission Statement has four facets:

1. They are your Marching Orders.
2. They are results-based (not process or features— results!).
3. People know what business you're in after reading it.
4. People can know by reading it if you're fulfilling your mission—it is self-measuring.

It answers the Big What in your business: What do I do?

Lewis & Clark were the great explorers known best for finding a passage via the northwest to the Pacific Ocean. If they were to write their Vision Statement today (assuming they had watched a few Star Trek flicks), their Vision Statement might be:

"Going where no man has gone before."

It doesn't necessarily tell you what they do, but they wouldn't have written that for you. They know what it means—they're pioneers at heart and find great joy in getting out of bed in the morning to discover places others would like to avoid.

But their Mission Statement, written for their customers (the U.S. Government), would read something like this:

"To discover a passage to the Pacific Ocean via the Northwest, and map this for all future generations."

How does it do against the four simple tests? There is no question after reading their Mission Statement that you know:

1. Their Marching Orders: Find a way to the ocean via the northwest.
2. The results they will get their customer: Find a way to the ocean via the northwest and map it.

And if you are the U.S. Government (their customer), after reading it you will know:

3. What business they are in: Pioneering new frontiers and mapping them.

And if they will accomplish it:

4. Did they discover a passage and map it? Yes.

—you will measure the success of your Mission by what your clients experience, obtain, receive, etc.   Write in terms of *results*

Again, the Vision is WHY you exist (your motivator); the Mission is WHAT you will actually do as a company; and the RESULT is what you provide for yourself and your clients.

When people finish reading your Vision Statement, they should know what motivates you. But when they finish reading your Mission Statement, they should know exactly what they are going to get out of a relationship with you. The Vision Statement is all about you and your company; the Mission Statement is totally about your customers and the results you will get them.

VISION	MISSION
Values-based	Action-based
Why you exist	What you do
General	Specific
It's about you	It's about your customers
Motivational	Marching orders
General/ethereal results	Specific product/service results

My Mission Statement

Here's mine, which I would still like to shorten after all these years (A Strategic Plan is living and dynamic—it should always be tweaked!):

Helping business owners make more money in less time, get off the treadmill, and get back to the passion that brought them into business, so they can build a mature business in support of their lifetime goals.

It's shorter than it used to be, but I'd love it if I could get it from 5 to 15 words. Someday it might come clear to me how to do that and still communicate clearly the result our clients will get from relating to The Crankset Group.

No Processes, Just Results!

Notice that my Mission Statement lists five results I get my clients, but there is nothing in there about how I get someone these results. We make this mistake all the time—we desperately want to tell people *how* we do something, and they simply don't care until we tell them the *result* we will get them. If someone is attracted to one or more of the five results I list in my Mission Statement, we can then have a conversation on how I could get them that result.

YOUR 1-3 YEAR STRATEGIES

Strategies   10 to 30 words   5 to 10 minutes each

Answers the question—HOW?
(Good for the next 1-3 years.)

Now that you've got a motivating Vision Statement and a results-focused Mission Statement as your marching orders, the rest of this is going to get progressively easier and progressively more tactical. Each step we take in building a Strategic Plan gets us closer to what we need to do today to build a business that makes money while we're on vacation.

The Strategies in a Strategic Plan answer two How questions:

1. How do you make money (the products, services, marketing strategies, client retention strategies, and operational principles)?

2. How do you lead your company, employees, and customers? What culture will you create (1-2 strategies here)?

Most of the emphasis should be on how you make money. You'll only need one or two Strategies on how you lead. In some cases, how you make money makes it clear how you lead both your customers and your company.

Your Strategies are your *revenue streams* and your *leadership practices;* it's just that simple. Don't torture this stuff.

I mentioned hierarchy before in building your Strategic Plan, but it's important to re-state it here now that you're into the process. Everything in the Strategic Plan builds on everything else that comes before it. Which is why it gets easier and easier the farther we get into it. We'll be doing a lot of correlating back to earlier sections to make sure you're not just writing fancy statements that have no bearing on your business.

As you develop your Strategies, you're going to have a tendency to make a list of fun things you enjoy doing in your business. Bad idea! Recall that there are Seven Elements of a Business—seven main things that are going on in your business whether you pay attention to them or not. The tendency is to major on the two to three Elements we really like and ignore the others. Our businesses will never grow up with that approach. It's like hoping for comprehensive fitness by doing only pull-ups. Balance is required in your Strategic Plan just like everywhere else in life.

See chapter five for more on the Seven Elements—they are also listed below for you to use in building your Strategies:

1. Vision & Leadership
2. Business Development/Research
3. Operations/Delivery
4. Finance/Accounting
5. Customer Satisfaction
6. Employee Satisfaction
7. Community/Family/Self (What impact does your business have on the world around you?)

You might have 1 to 3 strategies for one of the Seven Elements and 0 to 1 on the others, but consider them all as you develop your money-making and leadership strategies. I'm not saying you need to have one Strategy for each of the Seven Elements—in many cases you won't have a Strategy developed for some Elements because of where you are in your business cycle. But you should cover, at a minimum:

1. Vision & Leadership
2. Business Development/Research
3. Operations/Delivery
4. Finance/Accounting

Here are some additional questions to consider:

- Who is your main target market? Just express the broad strategies for reaching it/them.
- What are your sources of revenue— products/services (this is a mix of business development and operations Elements)?
- What are the few/simple strategies to deliver these processes/products/results?
- How do I turn clients into raving fans (customer satisfaction process)?
- How will you become the employer of choice (employee satisfaction)?
- How will you impact your lifestyle, your community, and your employee's lifestyles?

The key is to make sure your strategies are all going to help you make more money and/or lead your customers and your company. If a strategy doesn't have an ROI (return on investment), you're just playing office and you need to drop it.

All strategies morph over time, lasting just one to three years. How you make money will change with the market and as you get better at what you do, so keep to as few strategies as possible. Again, the game is not to uncover every possible stone, just uncover those top four to seven things that clearly make you money and the top 1-2 things that clearly help you lead your customers and your company into the future.

After developing your Strategies, test each of them with the following questions:

1. Does this help us make money, either directly or indirectly?

2. Does this help me lead my company?

Once you're done listing strategies, review the Seven Elements of a Business to make sure you have covered everything needed to build a business that makes money while you're on vacation.

Let's now turn to an example to flesh this out a little. Suppose we're going through the seven Elements and we get to Finance/Accounting—the first question we'd ask ourselves is, "How does Finance/Accounting help me make money?"

Consider a web design company that was constantly struggling, even though it seemed to have good revenue coming in. After some analysis, they realized that they would start a project, get way down the road, and then the client would cause "the big stall" by not having finished copy or design work. This stretched out the company's receivables because the projects couldn't be finished. In some cases, the client would even use this to stall further until they were ready to go live, stringing the web design company out even further.

The company decided that a good Strategy to solve this problem was to "Shorten receivables from 60+ days to less than 30 days." To accomplish this, they began to require that all design and copy must be in hand before starting a web project. The strategy worked! It eliminated "the big stall," created great cash flow, and even served most of the clients by helping them get organized faster.

Having a Finance/Accounting Strategy to shorten their receivables changed the way they did business.

Here are my Strategies, which by the time you read this have changed and morphed considerably.

Notice how I've related each of the Strategies to the Seven Elements of a Business. You should keep your Strategy sentences much shorter than mine. I can keep my arms around all this, but it would be easier if I would force myself to use fewer words.

Crankset Group
Page One – Vision, Mission, Strategies   Last Updated: xx/xx/xxxx

OUR VISION   Live well by doing good.

BUSINESS
MATURITY
PICTURE & DATE

February 18, 10am, 2011. Stage 6-7 business (continue in content development & delivery; others run the business.) $xxxk/yr annuity - $xk per mth to non-profit. Lv Denver 6:10pm; Arrive Auck, NZ Sun, 7:25am, 2/20/2011 $2,880 flights;$4,000 for hotels/trans;$2,200 food; $2,800 entertainment = $12,380

OUR MISSION   Helping business owners make more money in less time and get back to the passion that brought them into business, so they can build a mature business in support of their lifetime goals.

OUR STRATEGIES

1 INDIRECT REVENUE - BLI Lunches & Open Model - Be the board on which business people play and win the game. Invite everyone to everything. Live well by doing good. ELEMENTS 1, 2, 5, 7

2 DIRECT REVENUE - Mastermind - peer advisory, wisdom of crowds; One2One Advisory/Consulting - adds direction, intentionality, relationship. ELEMENTS 1, 3, 5, 6

3 DIRECT REVENUE - DYI Challenge (sets up FasTrak) & FasTrak - double your income in 90 days ELEMENTS 1, 2, 3; OnTrak – basic of building a successful business

4 DIRECT REVENUE - Workshops - a) Lifetime Goals b) Strategic Plan workshop - a mature business in 3to5 yrs c) Process Mapping d) Business Maturity Date Speaking - internationally ELEMENTS 1, 2, 3, 5, 6, 7

5 DIRECT REVENUE - Facilitators doing MM, FasTrak, One2One, Workshops ELEMENTS 1, 5, 6, 7

6 DIRECT REVENUE - Online Products/Services - Apex Profile, Strategic Plan, Woodpile Mgt System, FasTrak, and others. ELEMENTS 1, 2, 3, 5, 6, 7

7 INDIRECT REVENUE - Relationship Marketing a) Create Raving Fans of all b) Veins-credibility/motivation/relationship c)Hedgehog-outcome-based, no-nonsense; growing businesses to maturity, helping w/ a problem. d) blog/social netwrkg ELEMENTS 1, 2, 5, 7

8 DIRECT REVENUE - Book writing a) Bad Plans b) 3to5 Challenge c)Why Businesses Fail d)Apex Profile ELEMENTS 1, 2, 5, 7

9 We lead from experience, not from knowledge. Community; Conation; Lifetime Goals; Bus. Maturity Date; Strategic Plan; Waypoints; Serve, don't sell; Implement Now, Perfect as We Go; Outcome-based, Stage 6 or 7; YPH; The Priority of the Important; Clarity/Hope/Risk; Trapeze Moments. ELEMENTS 1-7

10 In each new area, will be grown into business, not go into it until it proves itself financially. ELEMENTS 1, 2, 3, 4

STRATEGIC PLAN PAGE TWO
YEARLY, MONTHLY QUARTERLY OBJECTIVES

Page two of your Strategic Plan is very different than page one. It is full of things to measure, timetables, numbers, dates, and other descriptors that make it clear *what* needs to be done and *when.* This is the part of the Strategic Plan that begins to pull the Priority of the Important into the present and give it the same urgency as making money. This page is the best aid we have for dual tracking—building a business that makes money tomorrow while we make money today.

I review the Monthly section on the second page of my Strategic Plan for 5 to 10 minutes every week, the Quarterly section for 60 minutes a month, and the Annual section for 1 to 2 hours per quarter. It's a very small investment of time to get great clarity about what I should be doing.

Nothing Urgent Goes Here!

It's very important that nothing reflecting the Tyranny of the Urgent appear anywhere on your Strategic Plan (with rare exceptions). How do you recognize what is the Tyranny of the Urgent? If the strategy, objective, or action helps you make money in the coming month but doesn't help you build a business that makes money much farther down the road, it probably doesn't belong on the Strategic Plan.

For example, say I need to change locations for my workshops next month. Should I put that on page two of my Strategic Plan? No, this only helps me make money now. Nothing in that action helps me build a business that makes money while I'm on vacation. But if I needed to review my workshop offerings to see which ones were most helpful and attracted the best responses, then that belongs on the Strategic Plan because it clearly will help me make more money in less time down the road.

Since you can't ignore the Urgent, you have to put them somewhere. I keep them on a task list, prioritizing them A, B, and C to make sure I'm doing the most Urgent things first. These things tend to come find me so I don't have to sit around and think of them, I just have to get them prioritized and attack them in that order.

YOUR 12-MONTH OBJECTIVES

Objectives   10 to 30 words   5 to 30 minutes each

Answers the question—WHAT/WHEN?
(Good for the next 12 months.)

Unlike the development of most Business Plans, the twelve-month objectives are not arrived at in a vacuum. The wrong question (the one used for most Business Planning) is, "Well, how much do you think we should grow the business this year?" The right question is, "Based on our Business Maturity Date and our money-making Strategies on page one, what Waypoint/Milestone do we want to reach this year to keep us on track?"

Answering the Two Most Important Questions in Business—Why and When

This is the page on which we answer these two questions and it changes everything we measure. Rather than growing your business by 12 percent because that's what some mega-business did last year, we have real reasons, real motivations, and real numbers for what we're doing. This is because we are not just answering a "What" question ("What's our growth number?"), but we're answering the much more important "Why" question ("Why do we need that specific growth?") and "When" question ("To keep us on track to our BMD, of course."").

And again, in a Strategic Plan, everything correlates back up to the section above it. One of the problems with Business Plans is that the Vision, Mission, Strategies and Objectives are too often written in silos, with little relationship to one another, as if the objective was to fill in the blanks and not to construct a meaningful, intentional, integrated plan. The Vision and Business Maturity Date informs our Mission, our Mission informs our Strategies, and all of these inform our Objectives.

So when putting together the Objectives, the first question you want to answer is, "How much do we need to grow this year to stay on track with our Business Maturity Date?" If your BMD is five years out, you can divide by five, but that's a little simplistic. It's probably better to consider what motivational speaker Tony Robbins, says: "We overestimate what we can do in a month and underestimate what we can do in a year."

The same is true for a five-year period. You might want to accomplish less of the growth in the first year and progressively develop more until the 5th year. So, at the end of one year, you might only be 10 percent to your five-year goal, but in the 5th year, you can grow by 30 percent and make up for it. We burn a lot of fuel on take-off——remember that when deciding what you want to accomplish in the next twelve months.

Once you have a specific growth Waypoint (remember it's not a goal—you only have Lifetime Goals), that can be your first written 12-month Objective.

Objectives vs. Strategies

For the purposes of the Strategic Plan, Objectives and Strategies are very different. Strategies are about how we make money and how we lead. They don't have clear metrics or numbers associated with them.

An Objective, on the other hand, should almost always be measurable, making it clear what result(s) is expected in numerical terms. Objectives answer the questions what and when?

Resist all temptation to use this as a checklist for the Tyranny of the Urgent as we mentioned above. Only include Objectives that will help you build a business that makes money while you're on vacation. If the Objective is simply something that will help you make more money today, but doesn't get you personally further out of production, then put it on your daily To Do list along with all the other Urgent things.

Don't clutter your Strategic Plan with actions that are going to come find you anyway. We only want the ones on here that are whispering in the corner and never get done.

Waypoints (or Milestones)

Remember that your 12-month objectives are your Waypoints along the way to your Business Maturity Date. Each Objective MUST have a date for completion (with rare exceptions: If you have a maintenance metric such as "Maintain 95 percent customers satisfaction as reported in the Customer Satisfaction Surveys," then the date for that would be "ongoing"). For the 12-month objective section, you should naturally attempt to make the due date 12-months from now for as many as possible.

Once in a while you'll have Objectives that come due in nine, seven or five months. If they don't really fit in the Quarterly Objective section—stick them here.

Use the following to help you more specifically in developing Objectives:

- What is your growth objective for the year (which answers the "when" as well)?
- What new infrastructure, employees, etc., do you need in place? By when?
- What is your revenue Waypoint for each major product or service? By when?
- What is your customer service, employee satisfaction, and community/family/self plans? What metrics will you use to measure results, and by when do you need to meet these metrics?
- What special major projects do you have this year (write a book, start an online store, etc.) and by when will you have them up and running? What metrics are you shooting for to demonstrate you're getting the result you want?
- What processes do you need to map and by when?

- Increase profit margins from ___ percent to ___ percent by ___ ?
- Increase employee retention from ___ percent per year to ___ percent per year by ___ ?
- Acquire competitor by ___ ?

Also, keep the following words in mind when developing an Objective:

- Specific/tactical projects (that help you build a Mature Business)
- Timetables
- Numbers
- Metrics/measurables
- Results!

After writing each objective, review the list of words/phrases above and make sure you're on track with a good Objective. Refer to the example at the end of the Monthly Action Plans section to see how I did this.

Correlation—It's Really Important!

It is critical to ensure you're writing a Strategic Plan that is integrated and makes sense. Once you're done writing your Objectives, correlate them back to each Strategy (which are numbered one through x), and make sure you're covering all the Strategies with your Objectives. If not, have a very good reason for not doing so. The example near the end of this chapter, shows how this system of correlation works—you'll notice that Objectives A through J have small numbers to the left of the Objective letter that match the Strategy on which they're based.

Remember, your Objectives *only exist* to help you live out your Strategies, and your Strategies *only exist* to help you live out your Mission, Vision, and Business Maturity Date. Make sure they are going to get you there!

YOUR QUARTERLY ACTION PLANS

Quarterly   10 to 30 words   5 to 15 minutes each

Answers the question—WHAT/WHEN?
(Good for the next 3 months.)

Measurable   Specific   Timetables   Numbers   Results!

Now we're getting down to brass tacks. The Important things are being brought into the near-term and are getting some urgency. The Quarterly Objectives should be fairly easy to develop because of the work you did on the 12-month Objectives.

1. Look at the first 12-month Objective and ask yourself, "Is there anything I need to do this quarter to achieve this? Many 12-month Objectives require our attention on a quarterly or monthly basis—don't wait until December to get things started! If the 12-month Objective will take twelve months to accomplish, you're going to need to accomplish one-fourth of it in the next three months. Figure out what one-fourth you can bite off and make a Quarterly Action Plan for it.

2. Create a Quarterly Action Plan that helps you accomplish the first 12-month Objective.

3. Repeat with each of the 12-month Objectives. You won't always have something to do each Quarter for every 12-month Objective—some of them can wait for a few months to get any attention at all. Just make sure you are getting started on them before they all come due in December.

4. Correlate the 12-Month Objectives to the Strategies to make sure you're not missing something.

Look at the example at the end of the Monthly Action Plans section. You'll notice a big difference between the 12-month Objectives and the Quarterly Action Plans. In the Quarterly Action Plans we assigned an owner for each Quarterly task to make sure it gets done.

You'll also notice that we correlated the Quarterly actions with their 12-Month Objectives. You likely won't hit every 12-month Objective in your Quarterly Action Plan, but you want to make sure you haven't missed something you need to pay attention to in the near term.

YOUR MONTHLY ACTION PLANS

Monthly   10 to 30 words   5 to 15 minutes each

Answers the question—WHAT/WHEN?
(Good for the next one month.)

Measurable   Specific   Timetables   Numbers   Results!

The Priority of the Important has finally become Urgent! Our planning has finally arrived back to today! Those few Important things that are going to help us build a business that makes money while we're on vacation are now clear and have been given some sense of urgency. We now know what we need to do this month, which helps us accomplish what needs to be done in the next quarter, so we can complete our 12-Month Objectives so we can be one year and $X dollars closer to our Business Maturity Date.

1. Look at the first Quarterly Action Plan and ask yourself, "Is there anything I need to do this month to achieve this? Don't wait till the third month to get Quarterly Actions done that take three months to complete. Cut them up into three monthly Action Plans!

2. Repeat with all Quarterly Action Plans

3. Correlate

Print the Strategic Plan and review weekly along with the 12/3/1 Plan.

The following is The Crankset Group's completed second page of the Two-Page Strategic Plan.

Page Two–12/3/1 Plan

Last Updated: 11/15/09

12 MONTH OBJECTIVES
oct 1, 2009–sep 30, 2010

1–10	**A**	Increase revenue from $xxx,000 in 2008 to $xxxk run rate Dec. 2009, to $xxxk run-rate Dec. 2010	9/30/10
4,8	**B**	Finish Book 1 - Making Money is Killing Your Business - November 30, 2009. Book 2 - Bad Plans Carried Out Violently.... By June 30, 2010; Book 3 - Why Businesses Fail by December 30, 2010	12/30/10
3–6,8	**C**	Strategic Plan online process live	6/30/10
2–10	**D**	Refine/complete Process Manual 1) FasTrak 2) DYI Chall. 3) Mastermind 4) Lifetime Goals 5) Strategic Plan wrkshp 6) Raving Fans Process 7) Business Profile followup Process 8) BLI Lunch 9) OnTrak	9/30/10
4–6,8	**E**	Strategic Plan online process live	6/30/10
4–6,8	**F**	Woodpile management system online/live	12/30/10
1–10	**G**	Customer Retention - maintain at 98% per month, Increase donations to non-profits by 200% over 1/1/09	9/30/10
4–8	**H**	Process Mapping management system online	12/30/10

3 MONTH OBJECTIVES
What to do this quarter to complete above 12 month Objectives

Which Objective above does each Action fulfill? Fill in that Objective Letter to left of Action Numbers below.

OCTOBER-DECEMBER 2009

			OWNER	DUE DATE
A–B	**1**	Complete "Making Money" draft—PUBLISH!	Chuck	9/30/09
A–B	**2**	Apex Profile tested and complete—get PR started!	Chuck	12/30/09
A–C, E	**3**	Complete all written material for Strategic Plan online version	Chuck	6/30/09
A,F	**4**	Complete Timeline (Action Plan worksheet) for Woodpile online go-live date	Diane	9/30/09
A, G	**5**	Add Customer Retention data to monthly Accounting spreadsheet	Diane	6/30/09
A, H	**6**	Complete Timeline (Action Plan worksheet) for Process Mapping online go-live date	Diane	12/30/09
	7	Annual Objectives untouched - D		

THIS MONTH'S ACTIONS
What to do this month to complete above Quarterly Action Plans

Which Actions above does each Action fulfill? Fill in that Quarterly Letter to left of Monthly Numbers below.

OCTOBER		OWNER	DUE DATE
1 **A**	Complete "Making Money" draft; turn over to others for review	Chuck	11/7/09
2 **B**	Complete nine final Apex profiles - go beta and give to others for review	Chuck	11/1/09
2 **C**	Get dates in place for Kevin's Benchmark Survey	Diane	11/1/09
1–6 **D**	Continue growing blog following; blog weekly	Chuck	11/30/09
1–6 **E**	Plan speaking engagements outside Denver	Diane	11/30/09
F	Review Strategic Plan specs and complete outline of the project	Chuck	11/30/09

Action Plan Worksheets

Many of your 12-month Objectives and even some of your Quarterly Action Plans (and fewer still, Monthly Action Plans) might be big enough to require division into bite-sized chunks. They're more like projects than simple actions.

If you have some of these, you can do one of two things. You can either put them into some complex Project Management software that will take hours to set up and likely never be kept up to date, because updating takes more time than just doing the project, *or* you can put together a simple Action Plan Worksheet from which to manage these projects. I vote for option two, a simple Action Plan Worksheet. Resist the urge to spend too much time playing office—do only what you have to in order to get the project done!

Some actions will require multiple Milestones over multiple weeks/months—these should be detailed out on the Action Plan Worksheet. Be selective, since not all Objectives need to be detailed this way. Have I mentioned that you shouldn't play office? You can waste a lot of time getting ready to get ready. Get moving on getting things done rather than planning how you will get them done.

If you do need an Action Plan Worksheet, the following might be helpful:

1. *Project description* (do a different sheet for each project)
2. *How does it affect the bottom line* (Return on Investment)?
3. *Measure success how?*
4. *Date—exactly when will it be completed* (day, not month)?
5. *Responsible party* (more than one person may touch it, but who is the project manager?)
6. *Budgets—rarely needed* (unless your project requires thousands or tens of thousands of dollars)

Action#   Date to Complete:

ACTION PLAN WORKSHEET
For Projects (not just actions)

Use this for Action Plans with multiple Milestones over Multiple weeks/months—**Projects**, not just Actions

S.M.A.R.T—Specific, Measurable, Achievable/Appropriate, Results-Oriented, Timed (dated)

ACTION PLAN DESCRIPTION (from Business Strategy—Action Plans Section)
PROCESS MAPS FOR ALL MAJOR ACTIVITY

What Impact would completing this project have on the business? Describe that result here briefly. Include ROI.

1. Consistency of experience for both clients and employees; 2. Ease of Training and distribution of responsibilities; 3. Better tracking of quality delivery

How will you measure the impact? ROI, RFPs, Web activity, phone calls, etc.

1. Consistency of experience for employees and clients; 2. Ability to measure performance in each area of our business; 3. Increased ROI from increased throughput

Once you have the big info above (again, you might need all of it), simply detail out the individual waypoints that add up to a completed Project. Then use this sheet to make sure you're getting things done on time. That's it—don't complicate it!

WAYPOINTS TO COMPLETE ACTION

Steps to achieve goal	Owner	Target Date	Completed On:
❶ FasTrack Process Map & Process Description	Diane	9/15/08	
❷ DYI Challenge Process Map & Process Description	Chuck	10/15/08	
❸ MasterMind Process Map & Process Description	Diane	8/15/08	
❹ Lifetime Goals Process Map & Process Description	Chuck	3/1/08	
❺ Strategic Plan Process Map & Process Description	Chuck	2/26/08	
❻ Raving Fans Process Map & Process Description	Diane	6/16/08	
❼ Apex Profile follow up Process Map & Process Description	Grant	4/15/08	
❽ BLI Lunch Process Map & Process Description	Diane	7/15/08	
❾ Online Apps - 1. Apex Profile 2. Strategic Plan 3. Woodpile	Grant	5/15/08	
❿ Advisor Certification Program Process Maps	Chuck	10/15/08	

And if you need to plan a budget for the actions, keep that simple as well.
PROJECT BUDGET

Item Description	Cost	Total	Comments

Using the Strategic Plan to Run Your Business

Remember, your Strategic Plan is Boss #1. If you are not using your Strategic Plan to make decisions every week and month in your business, you are not using it well. This should be a dynamic, living, changing document, not a dusty proclamation that sits on your shelf. Use it every day to build a business that makes money when you're on vacation! Here are some practical "how-to's":

Weekly—Once a week, block out 15 to 30 minutes (my recommendation is Monday morning) to review your Monthly Action Plans with this one question in mind: "What do I have to do this week to make sure this Monthly Action Plan is achieved?"

Then block out whatever time you need that week to get it done—IT'S MORE IMPORTANT THAN ANYTHING ELSE YOU WILL DO THAT WEEK!

Monthly—Once a month, extend your weekly Strategic Planning time to 30 to 60 minutes. Revisit the Monthly Objectives every month and change to ensure you are going to reach your quarterly objectives.

Quarterly—Once per quarter, extend your weekly Strategic Planning time to two to four hours. Revisit your 12-month objectives and push them back out another twelve months. This is a 12-Month Revolving Strategic Plan, not one that sits on your shelf until next year.

Annually—Once a year, revisit your Vision, Mission, and Strategies to make sure your whole plan is still pushing you toward your Business Maturity Date (Exit Strategy). Revisit your 12-month Objectives and push them back out another 12 months.

It's not how good your Plan is, but how committed you are to the Plan you have.

Here's a key thought for you:

No matter how much time, thought, and research you put into your Plan, it will never be "good" without being rolled out. Every supposedly "good" Plan immediately starts getting beat up as soon as it hits the real world. And it is the feedback from the real world that will actually turn it into a good Plan.

So stop planning to plan. Get a simple Plan in a few hours and get it on the ground and running. Once you have it there, you will then have a great feedback system for making it good. The best indicator of success in an early stage business is not how well you've planned or how good your market research is, or even how good your product is; rather, it is speed of execution. Get moving! Then let the world help you perfect your Plan as you go.

Like the Chinese proverb says: "The best time to plant a tree is 20 years ago. The next best time is today." Stop thinking about it, go dig a hole, and plant something that will help you grow your business.

Simplicity and the Priority of the Important

The biggest difficulty most of you will have with this process is keeping it simple and high level. Everything we've been taught encourages us to make it as complex, thorough, and detailed as possible. That is why business plans don't work, there's simply too much to get our arms around. Don't worry that you will miss details. The devil is indeed in the details, but they will come out as you carry out each task. Unpack the details some place other than on your Two-Page Strategic Plan. Use the Action Plan Worksheets and go nuts if you need to, but keep it off the Strategic Plan.

Congratulations! You've got a Two-Page Strategic Plan with which to run your business. Use it daily, review it weekly, change it monthly, and revise it quarterly. It is the second key to your future after Lifetime Goals. Process Mapping, which we will cover in the next chapter, is the third.

STRATEGIC PLAN ONLINE

As of the writing of this book we are working on developing an online Strategic Plan application. If you would like to be notified when it is completed, please visit *www.CranksetGroup.com* or e-mail the author at Grow@CranksetGroup.com. This will also qualify you for a significantly reduced cost if you choose to use the Strategic Plan online application.

Simple Processes— The Road to Stage Five Success and Beyond

8

Most of what we call management consists of making it difficult for people to get their jobs done.

—PETER DRUCKER

O nce in awhile Mom would tell me on my way out the door to school that we were having hamburgers that night. But one night, I found chicken on the table. I was disappointed by the switch, which was silly because I liked chicken just as much as hamburgers. But she had set one expectation and fulfilled it with another. I was an irrationally unhappy customer, but unhappy just the same.

Earlier in the book I mentioned a realtor who sold a big house because a friend had referred it. She gave that friend a very nice high-end spa weekend away. Her friend then told their friends about the great referral gift. They, too referred a big home sale, but the realtor sent them a big gift card to a nice high-end bath and kitchen store. The gifts were of identical cost, but the second couple was disappointed and never recommended her to others.

In both cases, my mother and the realtor didn't have a process in place to guarantee consistency to their customers. They didn't mean to bait-and-switch, but because there wasn't a simple process in place; they had set one expectation but delivered a different result…all in the name of trying to be a good provider and realtor.

But they were winging it. The realtor's first customer told the second about the weekend, but the expensive house-warming gift left the second customer feeling short-changed—the realtor had set an expectation for how they would be treated and then changed the rules of the game on them by getting creative. They thought they were getting hamburgers and they got chicken instead.

PASSION MAY NOT HELP YOU DO PROCESS MAPPING

Passion for what you do is a great asset in starting a business. It can get you through the tough early times when more money is going out than coming in. But that same passion can very often become a liability in growing your business to maturity.

This is because your love for what you do can keep you too close to production—one of the main reasons most businesses stall at Stage Four Stability. That passion can also make you feel that no one can do it as well as you can, which continues the Stage Four trap. Process mapping is one of the best ways to help you identify how your passion may be holding you back.

PROCESS MAPPING CREATES CONSISTENCY

People don't buy quality, they buy consistency. Remember, they make the decision on what quality level they will buy before leaving the house ("Do I want a high-end status car or an inexpensive compact, fast food or a rare T-bone?"). Then they find the place that delivers that level of quality with the most consistent customer experience.

Do you want a successful business? Stop focusing so much on having the *highest* quality and focus instead on a consistent level of quality. Process Mapping is one of the keys to that consistency.

In his *Third Secret of Small Business Success (of Four Secrets)*,

People don't buy quality, they buy consistency.

Brian Phillips says, "Consistent results come from consistent actions. Too often we fall into crisis management mode and the wheels fall off the cart."

ENTER EDWARD DEMING—JAPAN, 1950

Edward Deming, the father of modern quality and customer satisfaction, had an 85/15 rule: "85 percent of a worker's effectiveness is determined by the process he works within, only 15 percent by his own skill." For this reason alone, one-person companies need consistent processes as much as 500-person companies do, actually more. Without processes, I'm unlikely to be able to deliver the same high quality of work every time and training others to do it will be very difficult.

> "A system [process] is a network of interdependent components that work together to try to accomplish the aim of the system. A system must have an aim. Without an aim, there is no system."
> —Edward Deming

From 1950 on, Deming—an American—had more influence on Japanese production than any other non-Japanese person. He held near cult-status there for decades before companies in the U.S. listened to him. Deming heavily advocated well-described processes. One of his famous sayings is, "Every activity and every job is a part of the process," and at least two of his famous fourteen management principles call for Process Mapping as well:

- *Deming Principle # 2*—Cease dependence on inspection to achieve quality. Eliminate the need for inspection on a mass basis by building quality into the product in the first place.

- *Deming Principle # 5*—Improve constantly and forever, the system of production and service, to improve quality and productivity, and thus constantly decrease cost.

In 1982 Ford Motor Company finally got the picture and hired Deming to help them reinvent their company, which had a bad reputation for low quality and had lost $3 billion from 1979 to 1982. By 1986, they were the most profitable American auto company, and for the first time since the 1920's, Ford's earnings exceeded those of GM. While all three of the American auto producers continued to lag behind the Japanese in some ways, Ford was clearly in the best position of the Big Three going into the recession of 2008-2009.

THAT'S FINE FOR THE BIG GUYS, BUT...

The top three reasons we don't think we need to be like Ford:

1. *Only big businesses need processes—my company is too small to need all that "organization."* Wrong! Operating without processes makes us reactive, but more importantly, we create inconsistent experiences for our customers, ourselves and our employees when we "wing it."

2. *Creating processes sounds too complicated.* Keep it simple—a few bullet points for each process, not a 30-page detailed procedure manual. Just write down what you are already doing, and decide whether what you wrote is really what you want to see happen every time. If so, you have a process. If not, you have a piece of paper that will go in a drawer.

3. *I don't have time.* You don't have time NOT to do this. Thirty minutes to three hours should be enough. If you have three to six processes in your business, and you dedicated four hours a week to this, you would be done in one to four weeks. You likely waste more time each month and lose more customers winging it than you would spend in one month mapping your processes.

WHY WE SHOULD CREATE PROCESSES FOR OURSELVES

1. *Effectiveness/Profitability*—Natural talent and sheer passion is not enough to run a business. All of us would make more money if we systemized what we're doing.

2. *Consistency*—If each of your customers (or vendor or employee) has a different experience, you're creating issues. Why not ensure everyone has the same good experience every time? Consistency builds loyalty. Inconsistency builds confusion and disappointment.

3. *Transferability*—This is a key factor for consistency. When Tom goes on vacation, or takes a day off or worse yet, leaves the company, the "procedures" in his head no longer exist. A good, simple, *written* process can be followed by the next person without dropping a beat, especially if you have cross-trained your employees so that more than one person knows how to do it.

4. *Profitability/YPH*—All this leads to making more money in less time.

AN UNMITIGATED DISASTER

Still not convinced you need processes? Suppose Ford lost 25 percent of all its employees in a single day. This would be disastrous for their business. Production would grind to a halt and chaos would ensue for weeks as the workforce is rebuilt.

Thankfully, such a scenario is very unlikely for a big company. But small companies experience it on a regular basis and do nothing about it.

If you have four employees and one that's been around for five years quits, you've just lost 25 percent of your workforce. Then what happens? You fill in, others fill in, people learn to do things on the fly that nobody knew even needed to be done. Chaos ensues for weeks while you interview, hire, and train the new guy on the fly. Most often, the training method is, "The customer called and complained. Let me show you how to do that."

"IT'S NOT MY JOB!"

As a former Vice-President of Customer Relations and Marketing in a company of 800 employees, I was always battling the "job silo" problem. People would do everything on their job description, so you couldn't really complain about their performance, and yet nominal performance and customer service problems were as regular as rain.

One day it became clear to me as I worked to get to the bottom of a simple but highly visible snafu. A design sample was supposed to get to a client by overnight delivery and the next afternoon the client had called to say it had not arrived—they were not happy. I talked with the Account Manager who had mocked up the sample. She had given it to the Project Manager; the Project Manager had given it to the Fulfillment Center supervisor, who had given it to the Shipping Clerk, who had called FedEx to come get it. We found it sitting on the loading dock.

Where did the break-down occur? The easiest target is FedEx, but it's not the right target. The problem is simple—everyone involved had done their "job," but none of them had seen themselves as part of something bigger than their own job descriptions. That night, when their spouses asked, "How was your day?" they all could say, "Well, I did everything in my job description."

NO MORE JOB DESCRIPTIONS

Process mapping isn't just the ticket off the treadmill of Stages One through Four to the freedom of Stages Five through Seven, it has other tremendous benefits. One of the greatest is, as your business grows and matures, your employees will view the world horizontally rather than vertically.

Job descriptions unwittingly teach people three things:

1. *Stop Thinking, Check Off the Tasks*
   It teaches them that success is defined by the completion of tasks and adherence to narrowly defined parameters of work. This teaches them to stop thinking and to simply work as if they were a machine going through a programmed checklist of actions.

2. *The Silo Effect*
   Because job descriptions focus on a narrow set of tasks to be accomplished by an employee, it creates a "silo" effect for them as well as for departments. Employees then live in a vertically defined world with clear boundaries that separate them from other employees who have tasks on lists of their own.

3. *No Ownership*
   Because employees live in a vertically defined world, they never gain a sense of ownership of the business and how they fit into it.

REVERSING THE DAMAGE DONE BY JOB DESCRIPTIONS

Process Mapping can get you and your employees past these problems. *A simple Process Map will show someone that they don't just have a job, but that they fit into a process with other people.* A horizontal view of the world, in which they are a critical piece of a much bigger puzzle, replaces the vertical world. The employee is encouraged to think and take ownership for the completion of the process, rather than the completion of their tasks.

If we had process mapped the big picture before the FedEx debacle, it might have gone like this: The Account Manager gives the FedEx package to the Project Manager and asks for an e-mail confirming that FedEx picked it up, providing a tracking number.

The Project Manager gives the package to the Fulfillment Center supervisor and asks him to send the Account Manager that confirmation by 5 p.m., and to cc: her. The Fulfillment Center Supervisor asks the Shipping Clerk to cc: them all by 5 p.m., and to call him if FedEx didn't get the package.

At 5 p.m. or shortly thereafter, one or more of these people who didn't get the e-mail from the Shipping Clerk would have called or walked back there to see what happened. They would have found the package and driven it to a FedEx drop box on the way home. This is quite a different result than what actually happened because now everyone is focused on the right question. Instead of "Did I do my job today?" as outlined in a job description, they would have seen a horizontal process map in their heads and asked, "Did I satisfy my coworkers—the customers I work with? Will they want to work with me again tomorrow?"

ALL THE RIGHT STUFF
In short, not only does process mapping get things out of your head and onto paper, creating a repeatable process and getting ourselves out of production, it teaches people that the result is actually more important than sticking to a narrowly defined list of tasks. The result is a horizontal view of the world in which the employee has a sense of ownership, is customer focused, and can deliver a repeatable, consistent experience to all their customers, internal and external, every day.

GET STARTED—IT'S NEVER TOO EARLY
Very few companies get a good start on processes until long after they are needed, which really puts them behind the 8-ball.

The best processes will be easy to expand as your company grows and more processes and procedures are required. If you have to throw out the ones you started with instead of just tweaking or expanding on them, they probably weren't good to begin with if they were used at all.

To get started, just map the most "mission-critical" processes. And, again, keep it simple.

I use presentation software (like PowerPoint) to create boxes for each process step. You can also use a spreadsheet, word processing software, or a big piece of paper. We'll cover this in more detail later, but here's a very quick example from Bill Weston's company, Weston Landscaping, with three full-time employees and a dozen part-time employees:

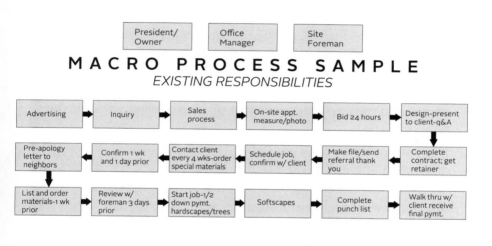

THE MACRO PROCESS

The above is a Macro Process for a landscaping company, meaning it is a big picture snapshot of their entire business. As you can see by the example, it is very high level. If your Macro Process has more than 20 to 30 boxes in it, you're probably showing too much detail. Keep it simple (have I said that yet?).

The Macro Process is the first Process Map you should create. Any others you do will flow from it, and it's also the best training aid you'll have for helping all new employees understand your business and, most importantly, how they fit into that big picture. A Macro Process will eliminate the silo and create a horizontal sense of teamwork right from the start.

But what is your Macro Process? Ask yourself this question: *What is the process of delivering our product/service to the customer?*

Map your entire company process (very high level/simple), from marketing and sales (or whatever the beginning of the process is for you), through operations and delivery, accounting and invoicing, to customer satisfaction. Include everything from the beginning of your company's marketing process to the very last thing you do to complete the process, such as cash a check, send a thank-you note, put someone (a customer or potential customer) in a tickle file to be called 6 months from now and so on.

Again, keep it as high level as you can and keep the wording of each title very short.

If you have multiple products or services that are very different, you might have to create a couple of Macro Maps to cover them, but try not to.

Resist the temptation to dive in and cut this up into smaller process maps until you get the Macro Map done first. Once you've completed it, you can create the three to five other processes you might need from it.

TYPICAL PROCESSES YOU MIGHT NEED

Once you're done mapping both your Macro Process and your other major processes, if you are under $2-3 million a year and have less than 15-20 employees, you shouldn't have more than 3-10 pages total for all the Process Maps.

I have listed a few you might need below. I strongly recommend that you get the first four or five as quickly as you can. After that, you can pick away at them over the next year (if you even need them).

- *Macro Map* (from marketing through ops, accounting, and thank you notes)
- *Business* Development (marketing, sales, R&D)

- Operations/Delivery (delivery of your product/service, manufacturing, etc.)
- *Financial/Accounting* (including invoicing/collections process)
- *Administration*—office management, production management, accounting management
- Customer Satisfaction
- Employee Relations
- Vendor Management
- Shipping/Fulfillment
- Procurement
- Subcontract Management

As a smaller business, if you end up with more then three to six Process Maps, you're probably playing office again. Yes, everything needs to be Process Mapped, but balance the time invested in mapping things that have very little effect on revenue with the need to build a business that generates it. You can always develop more processes as you have time and money to do so. Eventually you should have the whole company mapped. But not out of the gate. Pick your battles. And never create a Process Map for an activity you aren't already doing.

PARTICIPATION CREATES OWNERSHIP
I'm a big believer in the following leadership principle: Those most affected by a decision should have the most input. That doesn't mean they necessarily make the decision, but I'd be crazy not to know what they think would work best.

Therefore, if you have employees, don't even do the Macro Process Map without their participation. Have everyone do it separately and then come together to build each map from the separate ones. You are more likely to catch everything that way and you'll be surprised at who understands the different parts of your processes. And most importantly, it will create ownership of the completed map by those who will use it most.

TIME INVESTMENT—SHORT, SIMPLE, AND SWEET

If it takes longer than 15 to 45 minutes for you to draw a Macro Process Map of your entire business, you're either spending too much time on it or you don't know your business very well. Don't try to get it perfect the first time, it's much easier to get something completed and then throw darts at it. It might take your employees a little longer, but not likely.

How to Build a Process Map

Once you're done with the Macro Process Map, you can decide which parts of it you might need to make into separate processes. Some common sub-processes are Business Development, Operations/Delivery, Accounting/Finance, and Customer Satisfaction (one we tend to miss).

Step One—Write Down Each Major Step In the Macro Process

The Process Map is extremely simple: What is the very first thing in the process, what are the major steps in the middle, and what is the very last thing in the process? These define the length and breadth of the Process Map.

To begin, start at the bottom of a sheet of paper, and answer, "What is the very last thing in the process?" Write that down. Because we've done this a lot, I will say that what you write down may not actually be the last thing, but we'll fix it later.

After you've written down the last thing, ask yourself what happens right before that, and keep going until there is nothing else that happens in front. Many times we tend to map out only the production part of the process; don't forget things like advertising or marketing, putting the check in the bank, sending a thank-you note, or other similar things on either side of operations. Refer back to the sample, but know that it is not representative of the best map—there is no such thing. Just try to capture your process and map it in a way that is best for you.

Why do it backwards? Good proofreaders will read a piece backwards because it slows them down and they catch more that way. You are so familiar with your processes that you are more likely to skip major steps if you do it from beginning to end. It's not a big thing, but it will help you be more inclusive.

Stay Broad

Try to only put steps in the process that cannot be included in a broader step. For example, if you were a chair maker, you might be tempted to describe each step you take in making a chair. However, this map is not the place for such detail. Just create a step called "make chair" and move on. You can create a sub-process for how to make the chair later that will be extremely valuable in training others to make the chair for you. And for the Macro Process, advertising, marketing, promotion, and public relations could be all rolled into one step called Marketing.

Exceptions

One of the many benefits of Process Mapping is that it can and will highlight the parts of your processes that need the most attention, either because you've not trained for them well, or they are difficult, or because they are extremely important.

One business owner with no administrative help made a box out of "Put Check in Bank," because it highlighted to them the need to monetize everything they do. They could have easily made this part of a bigger step called "Invoicing" or something similar, but this particular business owner was really bad at charging enough for their work, so this was a good thing to highlight.

Have the Employees Do It Separately

As mentioned before, if you have employees, get some of the key ones to take a stab at the Macro Process on their own, then come together and create a master map from all the separate ones. Nothing will create a better discussion or reveal the missed steps in your processes more! It could be the most revealing and productive meeting you've had in years.

Map the Present, Not the Future

Don't map the future first, map the reality—find out what you're really doing before you decide what you want it to look like in the future. It's very important to face the music now, and it will be a great encouragement later when you can see where you were.

Yes, It's That Simple

I regularly get asked if this is all there is to it by people who actually paid me money to teach them how to Process Map. And the answer is yes, at least for now. There are some other steps to the process we'll cover later, but all of them are just as simple. Keep reading and you'll see the huge impact Process Mapping has on any-sized business.

Step Two—List of Sub-Processes

Once you've finished the Macro Process Map of your entire business, and before you try to fix any of the steps (remember, map your reality, not what you hope it to be), make a list of potential sub-processes that will have to be mapped. Try to keep it short. Take another look at the Seven Elements of Business below that we talked about in Chapter Five. In general, most businesses might need separate maps for Business Development, Operations/Delivery, and Financial Management. I'd suggest a separate one for Customer Satisfaction too because it is so neglected and is far and away our best source of future revenue.

As listed in Chapter Five, the Seven Elements of a Business are:

1. Vision & Leadership (mission, vision, principles)
2. Business Development (sales, marketing, research)
3. Operations & Delivery (get a process that delivers a consistent experience)
4. Financial Management (improve cash flow and profit just by paying attention)
5. Customer Satisfaction (almost no one has a process for this critical Element)

6. Employee Satisfaction (treat them like they are Number 1 and they will do the same for your clients)
7. Community, Family, Self (how is your business impacting the world around you?)

Don't Play Office

Sometimes you might feel there is a unique part of sales, operations, or some other element of a business that needs further mapping. Resist the temptation unless it is mission critical and helps you directly make money. You can always map these things later, but I can assure you that the more process maps you have, the more they will look like a training manual, and the less likely you will use them.

Step Three—Map the Sub-Processes

Once you've decided which sub-processes to map, have the employees involved in those processes create Process Maps for them while you do yours separately. Meet and combine the two to create the first draft of all your processes.

Step Four—Field Test

Have your employees keep the full Process Map draft by their desk or workstation for a week or two and ask them to look at it each time they go through the process, or at the end of the day. Have them make sure it accurately reflects everything they do.

Step Five—Meet and Complete the Macro and the Sub-Processes

Once you've all lived with the Macro Process and the sub-processes for a week or two, meet again as a team to finalize the Macro Process. Then meet with each individual responsible for the sub-processes and finalize those.

It's a great idea to get the reactions of others not directly responsible for the sub-processes, but who are still affected by them—you might find out why some things don't work the way they should. And those people can be more objective because they will have no dog in the hunt.

Input the finished processes into presentation software, or something more formal than a hand-written sheet if you can. Refer to the example shown earlier in this chapter. Nothing fancy, just something that creates clarity.

Step Six—Coloring the Boxes

Using different colors have your employees color each box based on who is in charge of what goes on in that box. Please note—the person who owns the box may not do any of the work in the box, but they own the responsibility to get that part of the process done. Try to push this ownership as far down in the organization as you can—managers should not own production boxes if you can help it.

Evidence of the Treadmill—Stage Four Forever

When Bill Weston first saw his company's Macro Process map, he had the same reaction many of you will have when you finish yours. You're likely to see graphically why you feel you can never be away from the business without something going wrong. If you are a smaller company, this process is going to make you nauseated, because it's very likely that, as the business owner, you own way too many boxes, just like Bill did.

This is the Macro Map of Weston Landscaping before we got things fixed. It's pretty normal for small businesses and clearly shows why making money kills businesses.

Now you can see why this is the first step in getting from Stage Four Stability to Stage Five Success and building a business that makes money while you're on vacation. Seeing one color (*your* color) in so many boxes should motivate you to figure out how to get out of some of the jobs that aren't at your pay grade.

This is the beginning of moving from a Stage Four business that is dependent on the owner for production, to a Stage Five business that has processes in place so that others can handle production rather than the owner.

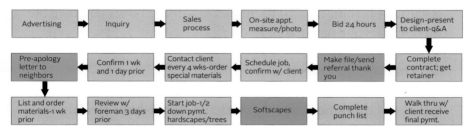

MACRO PROCESS SAMPLE

EXISTING RESPONSIBILITIES

Advertising	Inquiry	Sales process	On-site appt. measure/photo	Bid 24 hours	Design-present to client-q&A
Pre-apology letter to neighbors	Confirm 1 wk and 1 day prior	Contact client every 4 wks-order special materials	Schedule job, confirm w/ client	Make file/send referral thank you	Complete contract; get retainer
List and order materials-1 wk prior	Review w/ foreman 3 days prior	Start job-1/2 down pymt. hardscapes/trees	Softscapes	Complete punch list	Walk thru w/ client receive final pymt.

Step Seven—Assign Pay Grades to Each Box

Before we fix anything, we need to do one more thing—look at each box as a 40-hour a week job in a big company and ask yourself, "What would I pay someone to do this?" Put that hourly wage in that box. Then lay down because you're going to be nauseated again by how much time and money you waste by doing things others should be doing and would be glad to do.

You are an hourly employee—you should always think of yourself that way. If you make $100,000 a year but you work 70 hours a week to get it, you've got a pretty low hourly wage. Don't

MACRO PROCESS SAMPLE

HOURLY COST PER TASK

$12	$12	$150	$150	$8	$35
Advertising	Inquiry	Sales process	On-site appt. measure/photo	Bid 24 hours	Design-present to client-q&a
$8	**$8**	**$8**	**$12**	**$8**	**$12/150**
Pre-apology letter to neighbors	Confirm 1 wk and 1 day prior	Contact client every 4 wks-order special materials	Schedule job, confirm w/ client	Make file/ send referral thank you	Complete contract; get retainer
$23	**$12/150/23**	**$12/150/23**	**$12**	**$13/23**	**$23/150**
List and order materials-1 wk prior	Review w/ foreman 3 days prior	Start job-1/2 down pymt. hardscapes/trees	Softscapes	Complete punch list	Walk thru w/ client receive final pymt.

look at the monthly or annual income, figure out how much you're actually making per hour.

In a smaller business, you will see how many $10 to $20 per-hour jobs you are doing that should be done by someone else. It's almost certain that 50 to 90 percent of the boxes you own are way below your pay grade.

But I'm Saving Money!

This seems to make sense on the surface. Most of us make the mistake of thinking that if we do that $20-per-hour job ourselves for three hours, we've saved $60 that we would have had to pay someone else. But if we wanted to make $150 per-hour, we just lost $390 during those three hours.

If someone else did the $20-per-hour job, and you were freed up to do the $150-per-hour job, like generating new sales, you could have made $450 while spending $60 on someone else—a net of $390.

Stop being penny-foolish—Process Mapping will help you see the fallacy of doing business this way. Take the small risk of hiring someone else so you can get off the treadmill.

A very wise international, non-profit leader named Dawson Trotman once said: "Why do what others can and will do, when there is so much to be done that others can't or won't do?" What is the highest and best use of your time? Do that, and let others do things that are the highest and best use of their time.

Step Eight—Mapping What Should Be

Now that you're done throwing up over what you've been doing that others should be doing instead, let's redistribute the responsibilities to create the highest and best use of everyone's time. This is all about Yield Per Hour (YPH), helping you make more money but in less time, driving up your hourly wage with every step.

First, choose the boxes you want to get out of first and find somebody else's color to put in there. Do you still feel you're too small to hire an Administrator for 40-hours-per-week? Virtual

Assistants are a perfect way to start out—you can hire one for one hour or for 20-hours-per-week.

Do the same for each employee—if you see employees owning boxes that are way above or way below their pay grade, get that stuff moved to the appropriate person.

Once you and your employees are confident you've captured reality, you can ask, "What *should* this process look like?" Unless you've mapped the actual reality, this step isn't possible. You can't know how you want the future to look if you don't know what it looks like now.

Stage Five Success!

Here's what that Weston Landscaping looked like once we got done with Process Mapping. Notice the addition of a fourth person, the Virtual Assistant, and how the owner went from fifteen boxes to four. Bill Weston was ecstatic—for the first time in eleven years of business, Bill could finally see his way off the treadmill. He had a ticket to Stage Five Success and was excited to get there. And he didn't think it would take him more than a few months to do so.

As a result of this simple process, Bill was about to experience what few business owners ever experience—a normal business, not an average one: A business where the business owner is no

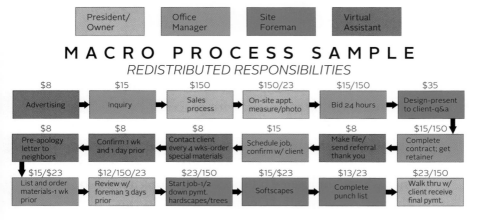

longer an employee of himself, and he owns a business that makes money while he's not around.

Step Nine—Assign a Cross-Reference Code to Each Box

You're going to need a code for easy referencing if you have more than three Process Maps. You'll also need it to complete Step Ten, which is the Process Description behind the Process Map itself.

I use a simple alphanumeric coding. So, if the process is "Business Development," I would label each box consecutively "BD1, BD2, BD3," etc. If it's the "Accounting Daily" process, then it's AD1, AD2, and so on.

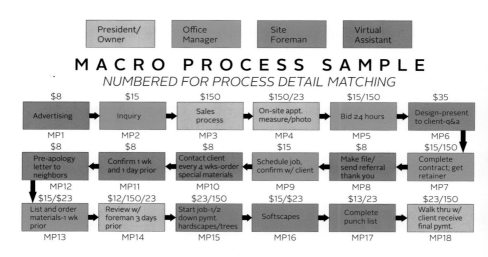

Step Ten—Process Descriptions

We are replacing job descriptions, thick and unused operations manuals and training manuals, with practical Process Mapping. In order to do that, we need to make sure that each person responsible for a box in the process can carry out that responsibility the same way every time, and train others to do it very simply.

Once you've completed a Process Map, look at each box individually and ask yourself, "Could someone do this task without more instruction?" In some cases they could, but in most cases the answer is "no." That's where Process Descriptions come in.

For each box, simply write out the process for that box on a separate paper. Don't forget to use the appropriate cross-reference code.

For example, here's a real accounting Process Map from Silas Carpeting, a wholesale and retail carpet company:

ACCOUNTING - DAILY

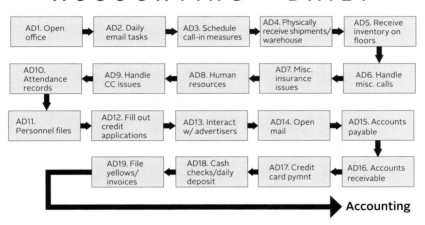

Look at "AD3. Schedule Call-In Measures." From that short phrase, only the person at Silas Carpeting responsible for that box would know exactly what to do. So we developed a Process Description that details what goes on behind that box. If you look at the partial Process Description below, you'll find the same title, "AD3 - Schedule Call-In Measures," and the detail of what the Process Map actually means.

You can see how valuable both the Process Map and the Process Description would be if Janelle, their accounting person, wanted to take a few days off. She can train someone else quickly because she doesn't have to remember each step, which would be very difficult because she's so used to doing it. And the person being trained will have this to refer to when Janelle's gone.

ACCOUNTING PROCESS DESCRIPTIONS
(Accounting Daily—AD)

AD1. Open office—Owner: Accountant
- Open up door and turn on lights
- Clock in
- Start coffee and cookies & put away any washed dishes
- Empty trash in kitchen and all desks and bathrooms
- Vacuum carpets as needed
- Put out balloons

AD2. Daily e-mail tasks—Owner: Accountant
- Go to Outlook Express under "Mail" tab
- Check any e-mails and respond as needed

AD3. Schedule call-in measures—Owner: Accountant
- Customers frequently call in to schedule a measure or "estimate" for their job
- If it is a new customer, inform them of the $35 measure fee
- Go to Outlook Express - Open All Public Folders - Open John's schedule
- John usually does measures on Mondays and Thursdays
- Ask the customer which day and what time would be best for them
- Click on the time on John's schedule
- On first line enter "measure" (carpet, tile, hardwood, etc.)" and customer's name and contact phone number
- On next line enter address and enter the sign " ~" and your initials
- Schedule at least 1 hour for a measure, more if it is far away or more than one room
- If there is a measure fee, go to FLOORS and prepare an invoice for the $35 measure fee
- Make a green copy and a white copy of the invoice—green goes to Carrie—white is folded up in an envelope with customer's name on the front
- Pull a measure sheet out of your supply for whatever is being measured (carpet, vinyl, hardwood, etc.) and complete with customer's name, address and contact phone numbers
- Go to www.google.com and click on maps. Enter address being measured as destination and our address (2095 W. Hampden 80110) as the "from" address. Print map.
- Assemble measure sheets, map and invoice (if any) and place in Carrie's Measure File

Figure Out What You're Doing and Get It Out of Your Head

For each of the Seven Elements we talked about in Chapter Five, ask yourself:

1. What is the process I do now for each Element? (You've got one, whether it's well thought out or ad hoc.) Write it down.

2. What part of that process is working? What isn't? Keep what is, and take your best guess how to fix what isn't. Don't spend hours or days thinking about it. Just change it. The only way you'll know if it works is if you try it. If it doesn't, change it again until you find the

right process. If it's broken, those quick "experiments" won't be any worse than what you're doing and will lead you to the best process.

3. Get others involved. Create ownership by having others take a stab at the processes that will affect their work the most. They'll probably know more than you do about it anyway.

4. Keep it to one page or less per Element. Resist the temptation to write an Operations Manual. It will sit on a shelf and you'll never use it. Some of the processes you write down should be less than half a page. Maybe one of the Seven Elements might take a full page, but see if you can't keep them to fewer than seven steps per process. Again, if you can't share the whole process quickly, you won't use it.

5. Prioritize the ones that create the most challenge for you. Get outside help if possible. Otherwise you're going to have to gut it out yourself and get them working in balance with the Elements you love doing. Until you do, you will be owned by your business. After you get all seven humming, you'll be on the path to actually owning your business and getting off the treadmill.

Keeping the Processes Alive

As with anything, you can't just create a process and ignore it. The simplest thing to do is to create a 30-minute quarterly meeting with the owner of each process and have them present to you the updates, revisions, etc. that were necessary as a result of changes in the business. It's your job to challenge those changes (or lack thereof) to make sure the process continues to be relevant.

Also, have employees stick the Process Map on their wall and keep the Process Descriptions on their desk. Encourage them to check their work against them regularly and suggest any changes that need to be made to keep current.

Keeping these processes current keeps your company out of an awful lot of trouble, and keeps the value of the company high.

It's worth mentioning again that Edward Deming said 85 percent of a worker's effectiveness is determined by the process he works within and only 15 percent by his own skill. How well defined are your processes? *Get good processes and get off the treadmill.*

Keep the Processes Visible

Print a big copy of your Macro Process and put it up in the lunch rooms and in the offices and production areas. Do the same with the individual sub-processes.

Laminate a wallet copy and carry it with you— pull it out to discuss processes with employees. Your process maps should be part of the daily fabric of your company.

And be sure to revisit and revise your Process Maps and Process Descriptions quarterly. Keep them up-to-date and let them run your business.

MAKING MONEY IS KILLING YOUR BUSINESS

Probably nothing demonstrates the treadmill effect of Stages One through Four better than Process Mapping. Most business owners never get off the treadmill because they never look objectively at what they are doing and see that they are simply employees of themselves, that they really don't own the business, but it owns them.

> Most business owners never get off the treadmill because they never look objectively at what they are doing and see that they are simply employees of themselves, that they really don't own the business, but it owns them.

I encourage you to take the few hours needed to process map your business and see graphically what you have created, how you can fix it, and move to Stage Five Success and beyond. In the next chapter we'll see why so few business owners take these steps to get off the treadmill.

PROCESS MAPPING ONLINE

As of the writing of this book we are working on developing an online Process Mapping application. If you would like to be notified when it is completed, please visit:

www.cranksetgroup.com or e-mail the author at:
grow@cranksetgroup.com.

This will also qualify you for a significantly reduced cost if you choose to use the Strategic Plan online application.

Why So Few Have So Much　9

We either live in a world of abundance or a world of scarcity.
Which one we choose effects every decision we make.

—CHUCK BLAKEMAN
FROM AN IDEA BY BENJAMIN ZANDER

I shared the Apex Profile with a retail business owner with seven employees who had been bumping along, breaking even for two years. Her response was, "Where was this two years ago? It would have saved me so much grief and turmoil in my business."

Another business owner came up to me after a workshop and said, "I wish I had known this four weeks ago. I lost my best manager yesterday and now I know why. I'm going to go apologize and see if I can get her back. I think I now know how to work with her to make us both successful."

I heard an interview with a nationally known business coach on the radio a few months ago where the most interesting thing said was—that only 3 percent of all business owners control 84 percent of all business income. The other 97 percent are sent scrambling to get their small piece of the remaining 16 percent.

Why? Why do so few business owners have so much more than most? Is it because the few are especially talented? I don't think so. It's easy to find people who are über-talented, but I know a lot of them who are dirt poor, working like craftspeople in Stage Three or Four Businesses, charging next to nothing and living hand to mouth. Talent isn't the dividing line.

Do they have a stronger work ethic? I don't think so. I've worked with many incredibly dedicated, hard-working Stage Three or Four business owners who never get past being the producer in their business.

There are a lot of other skills that the haves share with the have-nots. But I've seen three attributes in most very successful owners that others don't possess: Vision for their business, a good understanding of the systems and processes to get there, and the intentionality to do what it takes to succeed.

They have the vision to know where they are going and when they want to be there. There is a Business Maturity Clock ticking in their head. They utilize very simple systems and processes and avoid getting wrapped up in developing processes that will just be a distraction. And from the beginning, they fully intend to build a Mature Business, not just make money.

VISION, PROCESS, AND INTENTIONALITY

Tom Watson Sr., founder of IBM, said IBM was a great model of all three of these.

In the *E-Myth*, Michael Gerber recounts an anecdotal story attributed to Watson. He is reported to have said, "At the very beginning, I had a very clear picture of what the company would be like when it was finally done." He knew where it was going. Most business owners have never thought of this except in the abstract ("Wouldn't it be nice if…"). Tom Watson thought of it in the concrete, he meant what he thought, and he intended from the very beginning to build a great company. Tom Watson had no intention of being the producer in his business and getting trapped just making money. He fully intended to grow a Mature Business from the start, which is why he was successful doing so.

Second, he asked himself how a company like that would have to act. "I then created a picture of how IBM would have to act..." From the beginning he constructed the systems and processes he would need to get the company there. He created a picture (which is what a Process Map is) of how IBM would have to act. As we talked about in the first two chapters, most business owners make the mistake of thinking they will concentrate on making money for a while and think about building a business later, if ever. *Watson was successful because he was Dual Tracking from the beginning—making money, but focused on building a business that made money for him.*

And third, he said he "realized that unless we began to act that way from the very beginning, we would never get there." He acted like what he wanted to become. He was intentional. He didn't have to reengineer the entire culture and direction of the company at each step along the way, because from the very beginning he intended to grow a Mature Business and become a great company. That intentionality drove them to make decisions that would build a successful business that made money while Watson was on vacation.

Vision, Process, Intentionality; Tom Watson had all three. He knew what IBM would look like when it was grown up (Vision), he knew what they would have to act like (Process), and then they acted that way from the beginning (Intentionality).

THE BIGGER NEWS—WATSON WAS DUAL TRACKING FROM THE BEGINNING

What you've just read is part of the more well known part of Tom Watson's success story. But he also said something that never gets the proper focus. It's the one thing that brought his Vision, Process, and Intentionality down to a practical level and allowed him to build a great company. Listen closely to what he said:

"…each and every day we attempted to model the company after that template. At the end of each day, we asked ourselves how well we did, discovered the disparity between where we were and where we had committed ourselves to be, and, at the start of the following day, set out to make up the difference. Every day at IBM was a day devoted to business development, not doing business. *We didn't **do** business at IBM, we **built** one.*" (Emphasis is mine.)

Tom Watson was Dual Tracking his business from the very beginning. Sure, they needed to make money to keep the doors open that month, but the real focus in the business was building one that would make money when Tom Watson wasn't around.

A BALANCED VIEW OF BUSINESS

Watson had an extraordinarily balanced view of business. He balanced Vision, Process, and Intentionality in his daily decision-making. This is something that separates the successful business owners from the unsuccessful. And unfortunately I've found most business owners are not naturally balanced in their view of business. They either focus on vision, or systems, or day-to-day intentionality and "doing."

The good news is that I've also found that little if any of this imbalance is because of the DNA of business owners. We aren't doomed to be unbalanced by our genealogy. Most of the imbalance in our business is a direct result of our experiences, not our personalities. The way we've experienced life as well as business, gives us a view of business that is almost always incomplete.

But we don't see it that way. We think our view of the world is pretty comprehensive, which gets us in a lot of trouble. The big problem is we work from our strengths and don't figure out how to cover for our weaknesses. So we make decisions from an unbalanced view of business leadership and don't know we're doing it. But our business sure knows, and suffers. The reason the few have so much is because they've achieved balance in their view of business and their decision-making reflects that.

THE APEX PROFILE—HOW DO I STACK UP?

How do we get balance? The first thing we need is an honest self-assessment of our personality, our leadership styles, and our business ownership style. There are over 5,000 personality and leadership profiles out there, and you should check with your trusted business advisor or mentor to find the right ones for you. Stop winging it and figure out where the personality and leadership holes are.

I've developed the Apex Profile which, unlike personality and leadership profiles, isn't designed to tell you if you are an introvert or extrovert, or what are your innate leadership traits. The Apex Profile is constructed using the language and settings of the business owner, so there is no translation required from psychometric language to business language. It measures three practical things:

1. How you view business—through what "lens."
2. Where you are imbalanced in that view.
3. How that directly impacts the way you do business every day.

The end result should be a clear understanding of what I need to do to become a balanced business owner in Vision, Process, and Intentionality.

Ron Stenson had a small, twenty-person fulfillment center focused on sending out marketing collateral and small products for other businesses. They had grown quickly the first two years they were in business, but had stagnated the last three years and he couldn't see why. He and I went through his business owner profile together and found that he was heavily product-focused and just loved being out on the floor helping out in production. He considered it a great strength, and it was, but he spent so much time on the floor that other aspects of his business suffered greatly.

When I asked him where the business was taking him, what his vision for the future was, and how concretely he was pursuing that today, he looked at me with that here's-another-woo-woo-guy-I've-got-to-avoid look on his face. But he was also direct enough to just say that he'd tried planning ahead and it had always proven to be a waste of time.

I then asked to take a good look at his systems and processes to see if there were things there that could be improved to get him and his company out of the quagmire. About that time he started leaning toward the door and was not so subtly ushering me out. He had hoped I could help him with production, but all I wanted to do was ask questions about the future and his processes.

I asked for permission to be blunt, and since that was his style, we finally hit a chord. I told him it was clear why they had hit a wall, *because he was focused on today's production, ignoring things he could have learned from his past, to the detriment of his future for which he had no picture.* I asked him if he planned for vacation that way as well, just packing his car with no idea where he was going. He looked at me tensely for a second, then laughed, and we were on our way.

Over the next year Ron gained a clear vision for where he was going and why he was doing what he was doing. And more importantly, he picked a Business Maturity Date for when he would be there. This motivated him to develop some key systems and processes to accelerate the timeline for growth, and it helped pull him out of the production process so he could focus on growing a business that makes money while he's on vacation.

Ron had been very intentional, but lacked process and vision. He was typically unbalanced in his view of business and his approach to it. Once he got all three moving together, his business took off.

Don't focus on today's production, ignoring things that should be learned from the past, to the detriment of the future.

IT'S NOT YOUR DNA, IT'S YOUR EXPERIENCES

The Apex Profile was developed over time. At first, I just wanted to see if we could get a better handle on the attributes of a successful business owner. As I continued to profile my clients, and as the list of attributes grew, it became apparent that there were three distinct "buckets" of attributes. Most business owners had a Primary bucket of attributes they drew from first, a Secondary bucket of attributes they worked from less, and a Tertiary or Third bucket that often had very little in it.

I also discovered that someone's overall view of business and the bucket of attributes they used most were not really tied to personality. I've found raging introverts and raging extroverts who share the same Apex Profile characteristics. Your profile is an accumulation of learning—all of us have watched relatives, friends, and colleagues run businesses. Their approach, input, and feedback, along with our past experiences, together create a way of running a business that is likely unbalanced.

A FOURTH PROFILE

The buckets of attributes are actually three separate Profiles and I've found that, individually, the three Profiles are incomplete, that almost no one has a naturally balanced view of business. So, none of the three Profiles is better than the others—they are all equally imbalanced. The key to a successful business is figuring out how to get attributes from all three working successfully and simultaneously in the business. They all need to grow up to become a fourth profile, what I've so cleverly called the Business Owner Profile. There's an important reason for this.

Just because we bought or started a business doesn't make us Business Owners in actual daily practice. As long as our business reflects only one or even two of the three incomplete Profiles then we do not actually own the business—the business owns us and we are employees of ourselves.

Ron Stenson thought he was a business owner when he started his fulfillment business. He learned later that he was simply owned by the business, still an employee of it, and stuck on the treadmill by his imbalanced view of business. He got off the treadmill by doing what Tom Watson was so good at, getting balance between production, systems, and vision. He found his peak performance by broadening his understanding of how he viewed business. As a result, he became a true Business Owner—he was no longer in production and the business made money while he was not around.

Let's take a look at the three incomplete Profiles and how we can then use that information to become the fourth and "complete" Profile of Business Owner.

As with personality and leadership profiles, you'll find that you are a mix of all three of the Apex Business Owner Profiles, but you probably rely on one of the Profiles more than the other two.

WHAT IS AN APEX?

The word *apex* is Latin for *top* or *peak*. In bicycling, the apex defines the high point in a line around a corner that the bicyclist should take to keep the maximum speed possible and minimize the time they spend in the curve. It's the most efficient and effective route possible. The Apex Profile will help you find peak performance as a business owner, and create the most efficient and effective route to a Business Maturity Date.

MARKET, SYSTEMS, AND PRODUCT FOCUSED

The three average Profiles are Market-Focused, Systems-Focused, and Product-Focused. The Market-Focused profile reflects the visionary aspect of business, the Systems-Focused profile is all about processes, and the Product-Focused profile is all about producing products today.

None of them are complete and none of them are balanced unless all three are being used to play the game of business at the same time. We use the term "focused" because we want you to see that most of this is a view of the world we choose to take, not the result of the way we were born. We became focused on these narrow attributes over time and as they worked for us. But we can add attributes that we aren't currently focused on, and become better business people. There is no fatalism in this process; it simply reveals how we view the world now and what we need to add to create balance.

Many times we choose to add to those attributes by finding someone else who views the world differently than we do. This is smart business and I encourage you to do this whenever possible. But in a very early-stage business, it may not be practical to hire those attributes, yet if we ignore them, we limp along. Instead, we can choose to adopt a view of business and do things that we would rather have others do.

The following three descriptions are of each of the separate, unbalanced Profiles. Most of us draw from more than one attribute bucket to keep balanced, but looking at them separately is a good way to understand the three.

THE THREE BASIC APEX PROFILES

MARKET FOCUSED	SYSTEMS FOCUSED	PRODUCT FOCUSED
10-15% of business owners	5-10% of business owners	75-85% of business owners
Bus. Developer	Bus. Operator	Bus. Producer
Entrepreneur	Manager	Craftsperson

IDENTIFIERS

MARKET FOCUSED	SYSTEMS FOCUSED	PRODUCT FOCUSED
Customers come first "What do you want to buy? I'll make that!"	**Systems/Processes come first** "Are we doing the right thing(s)? Let's think about it!"	**Product/Service comes first** "I make great stuff. Somebody ought to buy it"
Risk Tolerant "We're making this up as we go along"	**Risk Averse** "How will we make sure it works?"	**Risk Neutral** "Today has enough trouble of its own"
Starting a Business "I've got this great idea for a business"	**Managing a Business** "I've got this great idea for operations."	**Producing a Business** "I'm making my product better and better."
Focused on the Future "Next year will be a great year for us."	**Focused on the Past** "Last year was a great year for us"	**Focused on the Present** "What needs to be done today?"
Action without Planning the Present "Let's do this before somebody else does."	**Research/Planning without Action** "I've got this great idea for operations."	**Action with Planning the Future** "Keep your nose to the grindstone."
Decisions on Intuition/Future "This could be great for our future."	**Decisions on Research/History** "This is what worked in the past."	**Decisions on the Concrete/Today** "What we're doing today works fine."
Enjoys Variation in Work "I've got ten great things going at once."	**Enjoys Stability in Work** "I really enjoy my daily work routine."	**Enjoys Producing/Making in Work** "I get better at producing everyday."
Starting "I'll finish this later. Got another idea."	**Maintaining** "We're getting this really dialed in."	**Finishing** "I've got 30 more minutes to work today."
Info Experiencer "What a great week that was."	**Info Gatherer** "What a great book that was."	**Info User** "What a great product change this is."

THE THREE BASIC APEX PROFILES

MARKET FOCUSED	SYSTEMS FOCUSED	PRODUCT FOCUSED
10-15% of business owners	*5-10% of business owners*	*75-85% of business owners*
Bus. Developer	Bus. Operator	Bus. Producer
Entrepreneur	Manager	Craftsperson
CHALLENGES		
Lacks Focus *"Hey, Look! A shiny object!"*	**Paralysis of Analysis** *"Give me one more month to make sure."*	**Florence Nightingale** *"I would do this for free (I nearly am)."*
Lacks Organization *"We're making this up as we go along"*	**Lacks Flexibility/Urgency** *"Don't mess w/ my system, it works as is."*	**Lacks Business Focus** *"I want to produce, not run a business."*
Employees Obstruct the Vision *"What's to understand? This is simple."*	**Employees Disrupt the System** *"Stop thinking & just fit into my system."*	**Employees Lower the Quality** *"Nobody can do this as well as I can."*
Controlling Ideas *"Thanks for your idea. (Not)."*	**Controlling Process/Systems** *"Thanks for your recommendation (Not)."*	**Controlling Production/Everything** *"Thanks for trying to do it (Not)."*
Risk Tolerance Endangers Business *"What's to understand? This is simple."*	**Risk Aversion Endangers Business** *"Stop thinking & just fit into my system."*	**Planning Aversion Endanger Business** *"Nobody can do this as well as I can."*
Market Variety *"We offer four dozen different things you can buy."*	**Market Reliability** *"We offer the same thing we had two years ago."*	**Market Craftsmanship** *"We describe our craftsmanship because we're proud of how we make stuff."*
Manage by Abdication *"Got it? I'll be on the golf course."*	**Manages by Thinking Too Long** *"Just one more rock to look under."*	**Manages by Doing** *"Why can't I get away from work?"*

Narratives on the Three Basic Apex Profiles

Product-Focused Owner: *The Craftperson—*
"I make a great chair, somebody ought to buy it."

I had a meeting set with Jenna Washington, a financial planner with four employees, but she called the day before and asked if we could reschedule because she had some hot things on her plate. We did this dance one more time before she finally made the time to meet. During that meeting she made it clear that she had ten things pressing on her, was constantly tired, could never leave her work behind, and that the whole office was incompetent no matter how hard she tried to train them. She ended up doing a lot of their work for them and it was making her angry and resentful.

Jenna suffers from being heavily Product Focused. She lives in a world of urgency and "today" and never has time to look back or forward because today is so pressing. The Tyranny of the Urgent defines her lifestyle, and she has no time for the Priority of the Important because she can't see how it will help her make any money today. Making money is killing her business, and her personal life. It keeps her from being significant and focusing on the things she was made to do best. It's no way to live, but the majority of business owners are on this treadmill and, like Jenna, are too busy putting out brush fires to see that they aren't even involved in fighting the main fire.

Passion for Their Craft

Business Owners who are Product Focused are passionate about the product or service they provide because they are experts, professionals, craftspeople, artists and artisans; implementers, producers, doers, and finishers. They like being tactical, on the ground, and getting things done. They take great pride in the product or service they offer. In fact, in my experience, about 75 to 85 percent of all new businesses are started by Product Focused owners (as opposed to 10 to 15 percent by System Focused owners and 5 to 10 percent by Market Focused owners).

Passion for their craft is what drives them to build their business. Their creative juices are focused on developing their expertise or constantly improving their product. They are focused on the present, what needs to be done today, and on perfecting their craft. Product Focused owners love to get personally involved in the System and have difficulty giving production over to employees who, in the craftperson's opinion, might lower the quality. They are much more passionate about their product or service than about what the market wants: "I make a great chair, somebody ought to buy it." Customers can get in the way because they want to modify the product or service.

Living in the Present

The Product Focused owner can't see the need to waste time thinking about the future or the past. They act on what needs to be done today. Spending time building good processes that others could follow is a waste of time. The Product Focused owner acts quickly on tactical things without needing a lot of information or planning. They don't expend much energy on "strategic" planning or action. This is a great asset in getting things done on a day-to-day basis, but doesn't set them up for future success.

Selling Process vs. Selling Results—
"Marketing? My Product is My Marketing."

"The product or service itself is so great that customers will simply flock to my door." This staunch product focus keeps them receiving good feedback from customers about how to make it more sellable. This focus would feel too compromising to the Product Focused owner. Therefore, if they do any marketing at all, it is Product Focused instead of Market Focused.

And they make the fatal flaw of wanting to focus on how great their chair-making abilities are instead of the result it brings the customer.

The product focus can also keep them from planning appropriately for the future, for downturns or growth, or for obsolescence.

Welcome to the Treadmill

It's no surprise that the overwhelming majority of all businesses are started, grown, and run by Product Focused owners. They have fewer failures than Market Focused or Systems Focused owners because they get production up and running quickly. But in the long run, they have more failures down the road than System Focused owners because they don't get good processes in place to support growth.

The reason most businesses in America are stuck in Stages Two through Four (Survival, Subsistence, and Stability) is because most businesses are started by people with a heavy imbalance toward Product Focus—lawyers, doctors, engineers, artists, plumbers (not all of them have a primary Product Focus, but almost all of them do). The treadmill awaits the Product Focused owner who doesn't get the other two Profiles involved in their business.

Sub-Profile—Technician

I've found that there are two highly competent types of people in the Product Focused category—craftspeople and technicians. A craftsperson has a passion for what they do and wants their name on the end result. A technician can be equally competent but prefers to work for someone else, come home, forget work, and ride their bike. The difference between the two is passion. Craftspeople start and run businesses, live their lives through them, and find a big piece of their identity there. Technicians work for Product Focused Craftspeople (and the other profiles) and go home to do something else.

Jimmy Stacynksi was young, so his view of the business world hadn't killed him yet. When I first met him he was 27 and had already failed at three businesses and semi-succeeded at one, which he sold for a very modest profit, not enough to make up for the three losses, but darn close.

Jimmy was a great visionary and constantly had his ear to the ground, looking for markets that were being ignored. Because of that, it's no surprise that while he was implementing "the best idea he had ever had," he had four new ideas he was trying to find time to get off the ground. The funny thing is that I met him on a golf course. He didn't like to go into the office much because he would just get "weighed down" by all the details. He felt he did his best work while relaxing and having fun.

I talked with Jimmy's office manager, Sylvia, a few weeks later. She was about to quit because Jimmy's torrent of good ideas were killing her and constantly disrupting her ability to succeed at any one of them. They called him "Golf Course Jimmy" and "Jimmy New Ideas."

Jimmy and I had a heart-to-heart and I challenged him to focus, with the incentive "carrot" that if he focused for a year to 18 months on just one good idea and got it fully into production, it could possibly form the capital basis for chasing new ideas for years to come. I could tell he was feeling boxed in by the idea of focusing and we drifted in different directions. I heard through the grapevine about a half year later that this most recent venture had fizzled too. Sylvia was probably secretly relieved she no longer had that job.

Market Focused Owner: *The Visionary—* *"What do you want to buy? I'll make that."*

On the other end of the profile spectrum from the Product Focused business owner is the Market Focused business owner. They couldn't be more different. Business owners who are primarily Market Focused are visionary, business developers, risk-takers, marketers, salespeople, and inventors.

They have a passion as well, but not usually for a particular product or service. Their passion is usually for filling niches in the market or meeting customer needs, with little attachment to the product or service itself. Their creative juices are focused on figuring out how to meet needs in the market with new products or ventures. In a sense, their passion is more for the game of business, rather than for a particular business. They don't need to be experts or craftspeople; they'll find a technician (not a craftsperson) to produce for them whatever the market wants.

"Don't Worry—It'll Be Better Tomorrow.
If You Need Me, I'll Be on the Golf Course."

They tend to focus on the future, the possibilities of what could be, and future products and services. They often lose interest quickly in the present product or service, and leave it to others to perfect. Rather than getting personally involved in production, they have difficulty staying close enough and would rather manage by abdication. Employees and others are obstacles because they don't catch the vision fast enough. They want others to get it, and they want things done now—they just don't want to be the ones doing them.

Speed of Execution—Big Picture Only

The Market Focused owner acts quickly on big ideas that could capture market share, without the need for information or planning. Risk bothers them less than the other two profiles, and can even be a draw for them. They don't expend energy on tactical day-to-day planning or production, which is seen as too granular—real work is strategic, not tactical.

Response to Markets and Hope in the Future

This is their default business strategy—today may not be great, but tomorrow will make up for it. Their focus on the future keeps them from developing the people and processes needed to make today work. Market Focused owners start a business quickly, but lose interest in perfecting it, making it very easy for them to have a lot of losses before they get a win. Their focus on the market makes them likely to spread themselves and the company too thin, creating too many products too soon. Managers and employees feel dumped on with idea after idea.

Know thy Customer, Not thy Product
Their greatest asset is their focus on the market and on customers, willingness to change to meet shifting customer or market demands, their ability to see things strategically, and take risks to fill the need. Their challenges include focusing more on the market or customer than on improving their service, processes, and production. After the idea is birthed, perfecting it is boring. They tend not to be good finishers. They manage by abdication, which is not a good growth strategy. They are multi-taskers, taking on diverse tasks that can make them more productive, but also spread them too thin.

Watch the Flameout Rate
While the Market Focused owner seems to have a great profile for starting a business, if they are highly imbalanced away from Product Focused, they will start well and flame out quickly. There are owners in the business world who are heavily Market Focused, which is a good thing—a little goes a long way.

Business Innovation and Grand Slams
The Market Focused owner is the person we classically think of as the "Entrepreneur," and they get lifted up as icons of how it's supposed to be for all of us. The word "entrepreneur" by the Wikipedia definition, which I agree with, is a "person who has possession of an *enterprise*, or *venture*, and assumes significant accountability for the inherent risks and the outcome. It is an ambitious leader who combines land, labor, and capital to often create and market new goods or services. ..."

Inherent in this definition is creating new goods and services (looking for market niches), and accepting significant risk. Very few business owners have these attributes—most simply hang out a shingle and say, "Wouldn't it be great if I could make money doing _____ ."

We really shouldn't hold the Market Focused person any higher than the other two. They have just as many flaws. They also have the highest failure rate because they take more risks (big wins, big losses) and they don't work hard on perfecting as they go. Fortunately only a small number of businesses are started by Market Focused profiles, because fewer yet survive any length of time. Their passion for customers, the market, or finding a unique niche to fill, motivates them to want to make money from the "game," not from a special product or service for which they have a passion.

Yet Market Focused owners are the source of the most innovation and creative new businesses year after year, and when they get it right, it's more often a grand slam than the other two profiles can produce. Just watch out for all the losses in between.

Sub-Profile—Salesperson

The two biggest differences between a Market Focused business owner and the salesperson who works for them is the size of the risk they are willing to take, along with the breadth of their vision. It takes a willingness to live with risk and an ability to hope for the future to be a salesperson, but it takes a bigger dose of it to start from scratch with just an idea and spend your life savings on it. The true Market Focused person will take that chance. A salesperson will jump on board if someone else is taking the bigger risk.

System Focused Owner: *The Planner—* *"How can I make this work more effectively?"*

Gary Keeney was referred to me by another client who thought we could help him. We met and as he shared his business with me it was very apparent that my client was right. Gary had a great business concept which should have been easy to grow quickly. But he had been doing it for three years and was seeing almost no growth. It didn't make sense because the idea was so good and he had done a tremendous job of creating great systems and sub-processes for delivering a consistent and professional product to his clients.

As we talked through his business, I thought through the Seven Elements of a Business and realized that Gary had great Operations and Delivery, a wonderful Customer Satisfaction process, and even a great Business Development model. And while his vision was lacking, it didn't seem to cripple his business. Yet nothing substantial was happening in a business that to me seemed like it should have been at $10 million a couple years ago, not the present $450,000.

Gary and I went through the Apex Profile and it became readily apparent that Gary was highly Systems Focused, which made him risk averse, caused him to think too much, took away any sense of urgency to move forward, and generally blinded him to the possibilities of what he was sitting on. He was so used to planning everything to the gnat's eyelash that Speed of Execution was never in his lexicon.

Gary and I developed a great Two-Page Strategic Plan to create a sense of urgency about growing his business and started marching forward very intentionally toward an aggressive Business Maturity Date. His business grew from $450,000 to $800,000 the next year and $1.4 million the next. Still not the growth the business was capable of, but a real stretch for Gary—he was thrilled.

If This is You, You're Already Reading the Fine Print

Business owners who are primarily System Focused include people who are administrators, managers, engineers, systemizers, efficiency and effectiveness experts, academics, researchers, historians, maintainers, organizers and process developers/followers. They tend to have a great capacity for detail, research and creativity, expressed by developing systems and processes.

Driven to Excellence (Perfection?)

They have a passion for systems, efficiency, and effectiveness. Their creative juices are focused on taking production to the next level to create better margins, faster and higher-quality production, lower costs, and stable work environments.

Like Market Focused owners, they do not need to be product experts or craftspeople. They are experts in process improvement, systems, planning, research, and all the things that help us develop strong production, higher margins, consistent quality, and stability. When things are going well, or if change would involve risk, Systems Focused owners want to maintain the status quo.

Getting Historical

System Focused owners tend to focus on the past, preserving the past changes and processes that are already in place, and learning from the past that change can be difficult. They can quickly think of many reasons why new changes won't work because of what has happened in the past. They lose interest in discussions about the future and are concerned about performing day-to-day production without a good system or process in place to run it.

Employees Are Cogs in My System

They can also be more interested in their systems and processes than in the employees that run them. They don't ask what the market or customer wants, and they don't need to have a passion for the product itself. Their passion is for operations, delivery, systems, and processes to create efficiency and effectiveness for whatever product or service is being offered.

Slow, Sure, Stable

The Systems Focused owners rarely have a good sense of urgency. They may feel it inside, but it doesn't come out in practice because there are simply too many unknowns to move forward. They are great at maintaining the status quo, managing repeatable processes, preserving history, and perfecting operations. They tend to move carefully and slowly on new ideas, researching and pre-planning all facets before acting. As such, they are risk-averse, preferring the safety of the status quo.

Research, Planning, and Preservation of the Status Quo
This is their default business strategy: The pain we know is better then the pain we have yet to experience. Systems Focused owners rarely start businesses from scratch—there are too many risks, too many unknowns, and no processes in place.

Fewer businesses are started by Systems Focused people (5 to 10 percent) than the other two profiles (Market Focused, 10 to 15 percent; Product Focused, 75 to 85 percent), but a higher percentage of businesses are managed by them. They prefer to buy an existing business they can improve upon with better systems and processes; or better yet, a franchise with a great system already in place. But their focus on internal systems and processes can produce stagnation and unnecessary bureaucracy.

These Are the Guys That Make Businesses Grow Up
Their greatest asset is their ability to take a good idea to the next level, put processes and systems in place to create the best margins and a consistent customer experience, and an overall ability to create a true "business" from someone else's idea or craft. Without the System Focused profile, a business does not grow up.

Their challenges include being so focused on operations that they lose touch with the customer or the market's response to their product, moving too slowly on good ideas, lack of flexibility, over-control, thinking and planning too much without action, perfectionism, and living in the past ("We've never done it that way before," or "We've always done it this way before.").

Building a Business From the Inside Out
Even though the Systems Focused owner starts very few businesses, they are very likely to succeed when they resist the tendency to move too slowly, and use their eye for process to grow a great business. They take fewer risks but have fewer losses, moving more on sure things. They also miss great opportunities by thinking about them instead of acting on them. Their passion for great

systems, stability, and effectiveness motivates them to make money from building a great infrastructure around whatever product or service is being offered.

You Start It, I'll Make It Hum

When the Market Focused profile comes up with an idea that the Product Focused Profile puts into action, the System Focused person figures out how to make it all work to make money, so that everyone can say, "We're really efficient and effective."

Sub-Profile—Academician

The lack of urgency and the desire to have it all figured out before acting work against Systems Focused people starting businesses. These attributes are usually accentuated in the Academician. We had a neighbor when we lived in Connecticut who invested 20+ years studying a single cell related to muscular dystrophy and she was making a tremendous impact in the world around her. Academician's like her are very vital to the success of companies with a focus on research and development, but they are the least likely to start a business and not much more likely to buy an existing one to run.

Business Owner—a Fourth Profile No One Has, and Everyone Needs to Become

Tom Watson is my best example of someone who can naturally balance Market, Systems, and Product profiles, which makes him a true Business Owner. But most of us aren't naturally balanced. We have to work at it like the people in the stories early in this chapter. But if we can either take on these missing attributes or hire others to balance us out, we have the same opportunity to grow a Mature Business as Tom Watson did. And just as a reminder, *mature has nothing to do with size*. You don't need to build an IBM like Watson did. *You just need to be able to build a business that makes money while you're on vacation, at whatever size floats your boat.*

As we've seen, all three of the common owner profiles—Market Focused, Systems Focused, and Product Focused—are incomplete by themselves. The Market Focused profile gives us that visionary perspective Tom Watson had: "At the very beginning, I had a very clear picture of what the company would be like when it was finally done." But it lacks process and some intentionality. The Systems Focused profile helps us develop process—Watson asked himself how a company like that would have to act. "I then created a picture of how IBM would have to act…" But by itself it lacks vision and intentionality.

Finally, the Product Focused profile brings to us the sense of urgency, the intentionality to get things done today. Watson "realized that unless we began to act that way from the very beginning, we would never get there." But again, by itself, we have only Urgency, and no sense of where we're going (Vision) or how we will get there (Process).

All three must work together to create the necessary balance to build a great business, big or small.

If you can afford to hire the one or two Apex Profiles that are not your strength, that's a great way to go—bring in the person who already sees the world that way. If you can't, you're going to have to tough it out and work to create vision, processes and daily production/intentionality yourself until you can. You may not want to do things you're not good at and that are outside your learned view of business, but business owners regularly have to do things that others wouldn't choose to do in order to be successful.

So what does a balanced Business Owner profile look like?

Clarity—I Know Where I'm Going

Business Owners are primarily focused by long-term, or Lifetime Goals, and have a very clear picture of the Ideal Situation for living out those Lifetime Goals. They understand that the business is rarely an end in itself, but a means to an end. Business Owners use their businesses to create an Ideal Situation to live out their Lifetime Goals. They have a clear

understanding of the Seven Stages of a Business, which stage
they are in, which stage is their goal, and what they need to do
to get to the next stage.

Passion
They have a passion for life, living, legacy, purpose, contribution
to their community and to the lives of others, and for growing
a business that can run itself so they can focus on these things.

I've Got a Boss—a Simple Strategic Plan
A Business Owner runs their business from a Strategic Plan, not
a Business Plan. Business Plans are complex and are normally
put together to make a bank feel good. A Strategic Plan is
usually just one page, lives on the desk, on the wall, and in the
wallet, and is used every day to drive the business forward,
make decisions, and ensure the Business Owner is staying on
track to meet his 90-day and one-year Waypoints on the way
to achieving his Lifetime Goals.

Balanced and Focused On the Whole Business—Not My Favorite Part
Business Owners understand clearly that there are Seven
Elements of a Business that must all get attention in order to
grow to maturity. They have a clear picture of which ones they
are good at and which ones they need help from others to
manage. They work hard to get all Seven Elements in balance
because they understand that doing so allows them to make
the fastest progress toward their Lifetime Goals.

Simple, Balanced, Process-Driven
Business Owners focus on Acquiring and Retaining Customers
Profitably, because they know that the only way to do this is
to have a healthy balance between the past, the present, and
the future. They understand the need for balance between
the market/customer, the processes needed to run a business,

and the quality of the product/service itself. They have a special respect for simple systems, processes and procedures which help them create a business that will run itself. They have completed a System Mapping of all their major business functions so that when employees move on, the business continues to run without a hitch.

I Use Good Decision-Making Principles

Business Owners work from a set of decision-making principles that guide them to success:

1. Make more money in less time—Yield per Hour (YPH). They work to reduce their hours while increasing their revenue.

2. Focus on their Lifetime Goals, not just growing their business every year. They know how much they need to grow it each year and why, which gives them much more resolve, purpose, and direction for growing the business.

3. Work *on* their business, not just *in* it. To grow a mature business, they understand they must back away often and develop strategies to get themselves out of the day-to-day. They work intentionally to get off the treadmill and get back to the passion that brought them into business in the first place.

4. Highest and best use of time. Rather than getting bogged down in tasks that someone else could do, they focus on doing the few things others can't that will get them to their Ideal Situation.

5. Make decisions on where you want to be, not on where you are. True Business Owners understand

that measured risks are required at each stage to move to the next stage. The pain we know is not better then the pain we have yet to experience.

6. Bad plans carried out with total commitment many times yield good results. Speed of Execution is the best indicator of success. True Business Owners make decisions and move on them quickly. They live by this motto: Implement Now, Perfect As You Go.

7. Tyranny of the Urgent vs. Priority of the Important—Business Owners know that there is a tidal wave of things that will sweep over us every day that won't help us make more money in less time. The relentless, Urgent things keep us from paying attention to the Important things that whisper in our ear. Business Owners walk past the Urgent things to accomplish the Important things that will help them grow a mature business quicker.

I Am *Not* the Producer (or, I Can CHOOSE to Produce)

You can easily spot a Business Owner because the day-to-day production no longer goes through them, which allows them to take impulsive time off or spend extended times away from their business without worrying whether it will suffer.

Intentionality—Growing a Mature Business in 3 to 5 years

Business Owners do not believe it takes 20 years to grow a mature business. They believe that it only takes 20 years when you are passive and simply waiting and hoping for good things to happen, but it is more normal for a business to grow to maturity in three to five years when they,

a. have a clear picture of where they are going,

b. have a plan to get there, and

c. have a commitment to specific dates for achieving each objective.

In short, they are proactive, not reactive. They take control of their business and push it forward to maturity with a sense of urgency, because they want to focus on living out their Lifetime Goals in their Ideal Situation.

Trapeze Moments—Taking Measured Risks

Finally, Business Owners understand Trapeze Moments in their businesses that require them to take a measured Risk to get to the next level. And they are willing to take those risks. They don't race ahead of their business and start living as if their business was mature when it's not, but they stick with the business and are "ambitiously lazy"—working very hard now so they can work less later.

Outside Eyes

The Business Owner understands that the John Wayne "rugged individualist" is a bankrupt idea. Besides having clarity on their Lifetime Goals, and a clear, written Strategic Plan that runs their business, they get Outside Eyes on their business on a regular basis to make sure they aren't running into cul-de-sacs, making good decisions, and staying focused on the few things that will help them build a business that makes money while they're on vacation. They understand they are subjective about their business and objective Outside Eyes are invaluable.

A Stage Five, Six or Seven Business and a Life of Significance

The true Business Owner can go on vacation and their business continues to make money when they are not there. They have figured out how to make more money in less time, get off the treadmill, and get back to the passion that brought them into business in the first place. And they use their Mature Business to support their Lifetime Goals. Survival, Subsistence, Stability, and even Success are no longer their focus. They now have time to focus on living a life of significance and giving themselves to the things they were made to do best.

THE APEX PROFILE ONLINE

If you want to take the Apex Profile online e-mail the author at *grow@cranksetgroup.com* and request a one-time code be sent to you for the Profile, which you will find at *www.apexprofile.com*. This code will reduce the cost of the profile to only $10.00

PULLING IT ALL TOGETHER

Staying On Track and Avoiding "Average"

10

Twenty years from now you will be more disappointed by the things that you didn't do than by the ones you did do. So throw off the bowlines. Sail away from the safe harbor. Catch the trade winds in your sails. Explore. Dream. Discover.

—MARK TWAIN

Now that we have a vision for building a Mature Business in three to five years that makes money while we're on vacation, how do we get there? The Tyranny of the Urgent is waiting to suck the life out of us as soon as we put down this book. All this talk about the Priority of the Important will get washed away and this book becomes another shelf-help book, helping your shelf look good.

PRIORITIES

The best way to change something is to replace it with something else. If you have struggled with the Tyranny of the Urgent like most of us, it won't go away by gritting your teeth. And it won't go away by managing your time. I tried managing my time for a while, but I kept discovering that I had the same 168 hours no matter how hard I tried to manage it.

I finally stumbled on the right idea, and then saw that others had stumbled on it much sooner—we should stop managing time and start managing our priorities. As my mother said, "There's no such thing as an excuse, Chuck, it's just not high enough on your priority list." And it's true. We make time for the things that matter to us. Do you want to know what you really believe is important? Take a look back at your schedule and your checkbook and they will tell you.

THE BIG WHY—WORK BACKWARDS FROM THE END

It's a simple drum I keep beating because I'm so convinced that the simple things are the most profound and are the source of the greatest Wealth (freedom). The simplest way to get the right priorities is to know where you're going, be convinced it is the right place to go, and have a date for when you will be there. Once you know where your Bermuda or your Mordor is, you can then begin to prioritize what will get you there the fastest. Until you know that, you're shooting a gun in the woods and calling it bear hunting. Lifetime Goals are critical to the successful business owner. It's the Big Why.

MANAGING THE RIGHT PRIORITIES—BOSS #1

Once you have the right priorities, you need a tool to manage them or the Tyranny of the Urgent will swallow you whole and you'll never get there. Whether it's the Two-Page Strategic Plan I use or a similar tool does not matter, but you must have a plan that is workable and combines the future with the present, so you know what to do this week, this month, this quarter and this year to get you to your Bermuda.

OUTSIDE EYES ON YOUR BUSINESS—BOSS #2

No man is an island, and as I've said before, being the Rugged Individualist is the worst plan for success you could possibly come up with. If you don't get Outside Eyes on your business and give them the ability to tell you you're heading off a cliff, you're living a dangerous existence as a business owner. Many of us fail at business simply because we don't get others involved.

Get into a Mastermind peer-advisory group and/or get a non-equity partner to mentor or advise you in your business. Give them the right to speak to you and your business. ***Adults don't learn unless we are disoriented from our comfortable view of the world.*** Use your Mastermind to stay disoriented; know that you don't know much and need to learn a lot. Being open to help is the best safety net you have.

A PROCESS DOESN'T MANAGE ITSELF

Whether it's by Process Mapping or another tool you have found effective, you need to break your business down into manageable bites and manage those processes. Businesses don't run themselves, and a process that isn't managed is no process at all. Stay on top of these things by having a regular time scheduled each month to review your processes. Put it on your calendar.

KNOW WHAT YOU'RE GOOD AT AND GET OTHERS INVOLVED

While I believe you can take on attributes from all three business owner profiles as described in the Apex Profile system, you should never try to fix your weaknesses. All that does is compromise your strengths. There will be times in the first few years of business where you have no choice but to do the best you can to play all three roles—Market, Systems, and Product Focused; but get other people in place as soon as you can so you can get back to the passion that brought you into business in the first place.

PUT STRATEGIC TIME ON YOUR CALENDAR AND MAKE IT SACRED

Thomas Hartmann built a construction company in South Carolina that he had always wanted to take national. He never seemed to be able to quite break out of his local business. After a few decades, he decided to semi-retire and go fishing a few days a week instead of continuing to beat his head against the wall at work. Within two years his company was a national player, and he attributed it to having gone fishing regularly, getting out of the office, and being able to think strategically in a way that he hadn't when he was in the office fending off the daily Tyranny of the Urgent.

Maybe you can't afford to go fishing a few times a week, but you should at least block out a few hours a week on your schedule as far into the future as you can, and consider it immovable time. Look at it as a regular meeting with your most important client, which is exactly what you are.

Once you have a few hours a week to start working on building a business, you'll find even more ways to stop making money and build a business that does it for you.

GET SYMBOLIC ABOUT YOUR BUSINESS MATURITY DATE

Schedule a vacation around it, buy a suitcase in anticipation of it, and stick it in your bedroom. Get that champagne now and put it in the back of the fridge. Do the picture-board thing; put something in your wallet. Have a meeting once a month for 15 minutes with your significant-other or friends to talk about what it will be like to get to that day. Put a countdown calendar together and start marking it off.

Do whatever you can to make it a regular part of your every-day life to help you stay focused on the Priority of the Important. Along with this, make sure you have your weekly, monthly and quarterly meetings to review, revise and update your Two-Page Strategic Plan.

WAYS TO BUILD A BUSINESS THAT MAKES MONEY WHILE YOU'RE ON VACATION

There are at least six ways to make money when you're not around. Here are some ideas:

- ### *Talent*

  The painter Renoir bought his massive French villa with just two paintings, and he bought his car with a pencil sketch. If you have unique talents, then you can charge enough per hour to work very few hours. If you can make enough money in a few hours a month to satisfy your lifestyle, then in a sense you are making money while on vacation—sort of.

  There are a couple problems with this approach.

  First, it's a crapshoot to have your talent recognized at this level. Plenty of people try out for talent shows who think they are "all that," and quickly discover they are definitely not any of that. Becoming one of the best at something so you can charge heavy premiums is not something to be taken lightly.

  My sister, Virginia Blakeman-Lenz, has played viola at the highest world-class level for decades, playing with the biggest symphonies and in the most elite invitation-only music festivals. A friend of mine asked once how she got there. I said, "It's simple. She was born with world-class talent; then she practiced for decades as if she had none." It takes a lot of talent and hard work to build a business this way.

  Second, your business really never matures because it still relies on you to produce. If you get sick or injured or worse, the revenue stream stops. That's one of the risks of the pure artist whose business relies solely on their ongoing production for income. So you'd better have very good short and long-term disability insurance.

- ### *Employees*

  This is the most common way to make money when you're on vacation—buy someone else's 40 hours per week at a discount, and resell it to your customers at a premium. The difference creates profit for you even when you're not there.

The majority of business owners are Product Focused craftspeople (see Chapter Nine on the Apex Profile), and the craftsperson has a natural aversion to employees. We think there is no one in the world who can do it as well as we can, and we're right, as long as we think that way. I'm sure Mrs. Fields has people working for her now that are better at making cookies than she is, and Charles Schwab probably has many stock brokers who are better at it than him.

If you can't get over being the craftsperson and can't ever see having employees, than you will need to be committed to one of the other strategies here. But employees are generally the easiest, most likely way for you to build a Mature Business. My plan includes very few employees, however, so I'll have to chase the other strategies aggressively.

- ### *Develop Unique Products/Services*
  If you're not über-talented, and you don't want employees, you can create products or services that you can license to others to produce. Or you can franchise your services for others to deliver, or create online software, products, or services that need very little maintenance. This is really just another version of Option Number One in our list, *Talent*, except there is a big difference.

  If you develop a product or service that others can take and run with, you're not living directly off your talent like an artist or a doctor. In the case of *Talent*, you only get paid for each instance of performance, by the painting, by the surgery, by the concert, etc. When you create a unique product or service, there are a number of ways to make money from it without having to perform.

- ### *Licensing & Franchising*
  I saw a documentary on technology once that showed the co-inventor of Ethernet, Robert Metcalf, floating in a very large boat in New York Harbor. He apparently made a lot

of money off that invention. There have been many smaller technology breakthroughs that have made a lot of people a lot of money. If you can create something others will license from you, you can make money while you're on vacation via the license.

Sometimes the thing you created isn't an object, but a service. If you've got a unique approach to something, you can license the rights to others, or get them to buy a franchise from you. Doug Root owns *Jungle Quest kids indoor rock-climbing and ropes course* in Denver, and after more than 15 years of owning one location, he has sold a number of franchises around the U.S. It's a unique concept that would be hard to replicate without the franchise knowledge. But it makes him a lot of money while he's on vacation.

- ### Low Maintenance Products/Services— Annuity Revenue

If you can create something that people can access and use without you being there, you can make money while you're on vacation. My son, Grant Blakeman, created an online subscription tool for bands called *Backstage* to sell their song tracks. It's unique and takes a smaller cut than *iTunes* and others. When he's on vacation people are still buying songs—he's making money when he's not around.

The advent of the internet has provided a significant opportunity to develop low-maintenance products/services. It has also unfortunately spawned a new wave of get-rich-quick schemes promising untold wealth by cheap websites using words like, "amazing, secret, wealth, easy, passive income, and unique" in the pitch. Here's a tip: The two last words of a dying marketing program are, "Me, too." If everybody else is doing it (there are thousands of websites claiming they have the secret to wealth), it's probably not a good place for you to pitch your tent and expect you'll make money while you're on vacation.

Real Estate is another form of low maintenance product. If you do it right (get help!), you can create streams of annuity revenue that will still come in when you're not around. Same thing goes for stocks, bonds, and other forms of investments.

Annuity revenue is ongoing revenue that comes in on a regular basis, as opposed to incidental revenue that comes in only once, as a result of selling something, finishing a project, etc. Annuity revenue is a great way to begin to build a business that makes money while you're on vacation.

On a related note, I know a real estate agent who put together a really good web application for pulling in interested homebuyers. But after six months or so of following up on these people, he found they were mostly tire kickers. He complained about it to other real estate agents who said they would be glad to get those leads. As a result, he ended up making good revenue selling these luke-warm leads to others who were glad to have them. Sometimes we don't know we're sitting on a gold mine.

- *Partnerships*

  If you're not über-talented, don't want employees, and don't think you have a unique process, product, or service you can sell to others, you can go the partnership route. Three dentists sharing a practice allows each of them to go on vacation without the office closing down while they're gone. This isn't really making money while you're on vacation, but it can be a good alternative.

  Beware the partnership, though—it is very tough to make a go of it. You're usually better off hiring a few other dentists as employees rather than creating a partnership. In a partnership, there are just too many opinions and nobody is really in charge. Avoid it if you can.

- *Passive Income—Not*

  A word about passive income for all you dreamers out there: ***There is no such thing as passive income***. Strike these words from your vocabulary. Replace the word "passive" with "annuity," it's the closest

> There is no such thing as passive income.

thing you'll ever get to truly passive income. Annuity revenue comes in every day, or week, or month on a regular basis without the same amount of attention you must pay to standard income. You can get it from owning real estate, having an online product/service people continue to buy, long-term contracts with individuals or companies, longevity in the insurance or financial fields, and so on.

But if you're hoping to build income that simply comes in unwatched (passive), you need to adjust your thinking. There is simply no such thing as passive income. All income needs to be watched, supervised, managed to some degree, or it can get away from you very quickly. A big percentage of lottery winners end up in financial trouble and bankruptcy because they thought they had passive income.

Playing with the stock market is no different. Every few decades we need a good stock market crash to remind us that this is not passive income. Sadly, plenty of retirees have had to go back to work because they had not properly managed their investments and ended up losing half or more by taking the passive approach.

Annuity revenue takes less attention than any other kind. Shoot for that, it's the basis for a Mature Business. But get the phrase "passive income" out of your vocabulary and you're likely to live a more financially secure life.

• *Whatever It Takes*

Even with these measures, you will still face distractions, uphill battles, tough times, and sometimes simple boredom that will get in the way of pushing forward relentlessly to a Business Maturity Date. You need as much help as you can get. Start with The Big Why and your Two Bosses then build a 3to5Club with others who are as committed as you are to building a business that makes money when you're not there.

Five Minutes a Day

Over the years of stumbling through my own businesses and helping others, we have accumulated a long list of reasons why businesses work and why they fail. It's a book for another season, but one other thing that might be helpful is to start your day with five minutes worth of visionary time in order to give each day a context in your pursuit of a Mature Business.

Every day, take five minutes, maybe even before you get out of bed, to review your Lifetime Goals, your Ideal Lifestyle, and your Business Maturity Date, and get in the habit of reading a paragraph or two of something that will keep your head above the fray while you're body tackles the Tyranny of the Urgent that day. What follows are 22 things we've seen that we regularly need to keep clear on so we can keep moving forward.

There are 22 business days in a month—use them to start each day if that works for you, or just revisit them and the other thoughts in this book as you need to refocus.

- **#1—Don't let your Lifestyle Get Ahead of Your Business.**

Ask yourself regularly two questions:

1. Which of the Seven Stages of a Business is my business in?
2. What Stage am I living in?

We so desperately want to live in Stage Six Significance or Stage Seven Success that we can't wait to run off and live there even though our business is in Stage Three or Four.

Some people like to use the phrase "lifestyle business." That's a euphemism for "hobby." A true lifestyle business is one that gets you to your Ideal Lifestyle. Most people living a "lifestyle business" are nowhere near their Ideal Lifestyle.

> Some people like to use the phrase "lifestyle business." That's a euphemism for "hobby."

It's no wonder why so few businesses succeed. We're living two or three stages ahead of our businesses. Get back in there and pull your business along to the Stage you want to live in. It will work a lot better that way and you're more assured to get to your Business Maturity Date.

- ## #2—Stand in Front of a Mirror and Ask Yourself, "What would I be doing right now if I wasn't afraid?"

If you're not afraid, then replace that word with the word or phrase that is holding you back—risk averse, losing money, stuck in the day-to-day, angry at the world, trying to perfect things before I move on them, taking too many risks, flying by the seat of my pants, or stuck producing to make money. You might find a different word or phrase for this sentence from week-to-week, but it's a great way to help us do the right thing. Come up with something and run it by whoever your Outside Eyes on your business are, and then move forward.

Bob Parsons, founder of Parsons Technologies and GoDaddy says, "Get and stay out of your comfort zone." Ray Kroc, founder of McDonalds, was predictably more to the point, "If you don't want to take risks, get the hell out of business."

- **#3—More Often Than Not, We Get What We Intend, Not What We Hope For.**

We live in a world of instant gratification, get rich quick schemes, secrets of success, systems that teach us to sit back and "believe" our way to success, and other distractions from the real work of success.

But we know that intentionality is the key. What you really want will show up in what you do, not what you say. Take a good look today at where your time and money are invested and see if those are aligned with what you say are your Lifetime Goals and your Business Maturity Date. Put a plan in place to make the needed mid-course corrections.

- ### #4—Trapeze Moments—Make Decisions Based On Where You Want to Be, Not On Where You Are.

Dreamers talk about the future, visionaries walk intentionally toward it. What risk are you avoiding that you need to take to get to your Business Maturity Date? These are what I call Trapeze Moments.

I believe the biggest reason we don't take good risks is because we're not sure enough about where we're going and when we want to be there. If you have no clarion call for where your business is headed, you won't have a good reason to take risks. You won't even be able to identify a good risk from a bad one, making you all the more risk-averse. But if you know what the end game is, what your business looks like at maturity, you have a beacon in the distance that will guide you away from bad risks and give you the hope you need to take the good risks that will get you to Business Maturity.

I hope this helps you see how important it is to claim your Business Maturity Date. If you think it's scary to set one, think about how scary it is to wander aimlessly in the desert of business for 30 years and end up nowhere. Once you decide to claim a Business Maturity Date, you will see it is the opposite of what you thought it would be. It is freeing, motivating, exciting, and a little bit exhilarating. And it will get you out of bed each day like nothing else before has.

You're going to have to let go of something that is giving you security to get to the next step. What is it? Make a decision to take the risk, put a date on it, and go public. Let those who are your Outside Eyes in on the process.

- ## #5—Dreamers and Visionaries

Someone who can describe for me some future, hoped-for situation, but has no clear date for when they want to be there and isn't actively pursuing that vision, is simply a dreamer. A dreamer loves to think about the future and what it could be like, but there is no concrete connection between that future situation and the work that needs to be done today to get there. And a dreamer never puts a date on when they intend to get there. Intentionality is not part of the dreamer's tool set.

The difference between a dreamer and a visionary is that a visionary has already taken the three steps required to create real and lasting change:

1. Make a decision (stop talking about it, stop dreaming, commit).
2. Put a date on it.
3. Go public.

A person who does this has burned the bridges; they've put themselves in a position where that future reality is the focus of everything they do. They are actively, right now, every day, doing the things that will get them there. Until you take the three steps that create real and lasting change, and get moving toward that clear objective and date, you're just dreaming and playing office.

> A dreamer never puts a date on when they intend to get there.

• #6—Clarity, Hope and Risk

Clarity—Do you have clarity on what you should be doing today to build a business that makes money while you're on vacation? If not, check in with your Two-Page Strategic Plan, your Business Maturity Date, and your Lifetime Goals.

Hope—Wishing and hope are very different things. Wishing comes from dreaming, while hope comes from clarity of vision. A clear vision gets people out of bed in the morning because they have hope they can get there. Dreamers stay in bed and wish things were different. Do you have real hope? Do you see yourself as a mere shadow of your future self, as my friend Donald McGilchrist says?

If you have a clear picture of where you're going, you can hope that you will get there.

Risk—If you have hope about the future, you are more likely to take some measured risks. Stock markets go down because people are not hopeful and won't take a risk. Business owners stagnate and stop working toward an Ideal Lifestyle because they haven't described it clearly enough for themselves or put a date on when it will happen.

Risk comes from Hope, which comes from Clarity. Get clarity on where you're headed this week and how it all ties in with your Lifetime Goals and Business Maturity Date.

• #7—The Problem of Parachutes

Very small, early-stage businesses fail all the time for one big reason—the business owner is playing office. They aren't fully committed to what they're doing. They think the wise thing to do is keep their existing job and grow their way into their dream. It sounds reasonable, and in some cases it is the only right thing to do.

But more often than not, the net effect is a subliminal parachute jump out of the business when we hit a rough patch (which every new business does). If you were the only person on an airplane other than the pilot and they died, and you have a para-chute, what are you going to do? Bail! If you don't have a parachute? You're going to take a crash course (sorry) on how to land an airplane.

> When we have a back door, we set ourselves up for failure.

When we have a back door, an escape valve, an "out," we set ourselves up for failure. Every small business growing up goes through rough patches, and if we have a parachute, it's very tempting to bail.

Burn the ship that carried you to your business as soon as you can. You're much more likely to make it.

- ### #8—Pursue the Simple, Run From the Complex.

Ockham's Razor says that given two possible answers to a problem, the simpler one is usually right. If we applied this ancient idea to business, we'd make a lot more money.

I find that business owners who succeed know how to sift through the Tyranny of the Urgent and focus on the Priority of the Important. To that end, it almost always seems that the Simple things are what make us successful, and the Complex things are what make us busy.

The Simple things make us successful. The Complex things make us busy.

The irony is that the Simple things more often than not are hard to do, and the Complex things are easy to do.

The Complex things are where I hide. When faced with some simple thing that will make me money, but it's something I find hard to do, I look around for some Complex thing that will waste my time but make me feel I'm being productive. Successful business owners know what the Simple things are that will push them forward, and they focus their time and attention there.

Managers deal with the Complex; leaders deal with the Simple. Lead your business—stay focused on those few simple things that will make you more money in less time.

• #9—John Wayne Rides Again: the Rugged Individualist

It's a myth.

Show me one place in society where we regularly practice this lifestyle outside of business ownership and I'll eat my hat.

You get married and you have instant community. You move into a neighborhood and you have more community. You buy a bicycle and join a bicycling club for more com-munity. You join the golf club and get even more. Then you start your business and you're on your own—good luck with that.

Meerkats live in community. Shouldn't you?

It's just crazy. Where did the idea come from that business ownership requires you to be "the eagle that flies alone?" With rare exceptions, the most successful business owners all have Outside Eyes on their business—people who can speak to their leadership style, decision-making practices, and direction—and help them get where they need to go. If you think you can go it alone, I can introduce you to an awful lot of people who wish they hadn't tried it that way.

You don't know everything; you haven't experienced everything. Books give us information, not knowledge. Knowledge comes with experience, and wisdom comes from an awful lot of experience. I desperately need ongoing Outside Eyes on my business.

John Wayne is dead, may he rest in peace. The rugged individualist should have been buried with him. We would all have better businesses.

• #10—"I Love What I Do" (That's a Problem)

Translation: "I don't want to build a business, because then I won't be able to practice my craft…I'll be too busy running a business."

Frank Gehry, the world-famous architect, is my hero on this one. Frank has built a great architectural firm, but rather than being the guy who sits behind the walnut desk and looks at spreadsheets, he's got somebody else doing that. As a result of building a Mature Business, Frank Gehry gets to choose what to do with his time. The documentary I saw on him shows him spending a lot of time playing with clay, shaping it, stepping away from it, and tweaking it. When he's done, he takes it to one of his employees and says, "Here, build this." Then he's on to the next lump of clay.

Build a business that allows you to do the few things you love.

The point? If you take the time to build a Mature Business, and you love being the craftsperson, you can design your business (you're the owner!) in such a way that you get to spend more time crafting than you have ever been able to in the past.

Building a business does not have to mean the end of you being the craftsperson. It could mean you get to do a lot more of it. Most importantly, it means you are now wealthy, not just rich, because now you can choose what to do with your time. Produce if you want, play golf if you want, spend time in your charity if you want.

- #11—Control

I have to address this as a reason why businesses don't grow up, but it's annoying to do so. We just shouldn't be struggling with this one, but unfortunately most of us do, and it is a contributing factor as to why businesses fail. We think there isn't another person in the world that could do it as well as we do.

Get over it.

Want to build a business that makes money while you're on vacation? You're going to have to grow up along with your business and give away the things that others are better at, so you can be free to do the things you excel at doing.

Being a control freak is actually one of the biggest reasons why businesses never grow to Maturity. The Product Focused craftsperson thinks nobody can do it as well as they can, and they prove it by killing their employees, making sure they are poorly trained, their

> We waste a lot of time proving no one can do it as good as we can.

processes are badly defined, and so on. The sad thing is that most businesses are started by Product Focused craftspeople.

If you want a mom and pop store for forty years that you can only sell for its assets and customer list, then keep right on controlling everything. Otherwise, go back and read the chapters on the Apex Profile, Process Mapping, and How to Get Off the Treadmill and figure out what is the best use of your time. You'll have a lot more fun building a business that makes money when you're on vacation, than actually making money yourself.

• #12—Ongoing and Intentional Confusion—Victimology

This one is fascinating. It's much easier to write about it in a book than it is to confront it in a business owner. One of the reasons businesses fail is that we subconsciously, yet intentionally, remain confused. No matter how someone tries to bring clarity to the situation, yours is somehow a special, unique, one-of-a-kind situation that no one could possibly solve.

I've dealt with a lot of these business owners and it is the toughest mindset to change. As long as I'm confused, I don't have to be responsible. It's the victim's mindset—there are 32 reasons outside my control why I can't figure out how to be successful. And as long as I can't figure them out, I'm just a victim of my special, unique, and one-of-a-kind circumstances.

Circumstances do not make us who we are, how we respond does.

Intentionality is very important. Have I said that yet? If you intend to get clarity on where you and your business are going, and when you want to be there, you can do that. If you intend, even subconsciously, to remain confused, you will. But know this—your situation is not special, unique, or one-of-a-kind. We never

Find others who have met greater adversity than you and have succeeded. Imitate them.

have to look far to find people who have met greater adversity than us, and it's pretty easy to find people like us who have succeeded where we haven't.

• #13—Fear of the Possible

Fear of failure is a big reason we fail to grow a business to Maturity. But the sad fact is if you never try because you are afraid you might fail, you have already failed. So don't allow yourself the luxury of thinking you haven't failed simply because you haven't tried.

There are two kinds of fear in the world.

Fear of the possible.

And

Fear of the probable.

You should fear things that are probable, not those that are possible. If you fear the possible, you will never go hiking anywhere that a bear might live, because it's possible a bear could harm you. If you fear the probable while you're hiking and you see a bear in front of you, you get the heck out of there.

Fear of the possible is paralyzing, fear of the probable is freeing and keeps us from doing stupid stuff. Fear of the possible keeps us from ever seeing the world as it really is because it's possible the airplane I'm on might be the one in thousands that doesn't make it. Fear of the probable keeps us from putting ourselves in imminent danger either personally or as a business; it actually helps to keep us moving forward, growing, and fixed on our Lifetime Goals.

> Fear only the probable, never the possible.

• #14a—Fear of Success

One other subset of fear is that strange, but not so uncommon, fear of success. What if I actually make it? Will that put too much pressure on me? Will my failures just be all that more visible to the world around me? I kind of like making mistakes in a microcosm—I'll just keep my Tinker's Shop and not try to do anything significant with my life.

If you fear success, your Big Why isn't big enough or clear enough.

I can't help you with this. I can only help you face it and decide if you want to push through it. I can suggest that if your Lifetime Goals, Ideal Lifestyle, and Business Maturity Date aren't clear and compelling for you, any fear of success will override them all. Remember, Clarity brings Hope, and Hope helps us take the Risk to be successful. A vision for your life can help you overcome the fear of success.

• #14b—Fear Leading to Failure

Let me give you something probable that you should fear: It is probable that if you don't a) decide to do something, b) put a date on it, and c) go public, that you will never achieve anything of significance, simply because you never intended to. That is something to fear.

If you try to achieve something, it's possible you won't. If you don't try, it's much more probable (100 percent?) that you won't. And again, your lack of decision becomes a decision—you've chosen fear and failure over risk and reward.

> A man still finds his destiny on the path he chose to avoid it.

It's worth saying again—A man still finds his destiny on the path he chose to avoid it.

• #15—Fear of Not Knowing Every Step of the Way

It is very clear to me what Maturity means to my business on February 18, 2011 at 10 a.m. Does that mean I have all the details figured out? Quite the contrary. I'm guessing I'll look back and laugh at some of the projections, some of the things we thought would be big, and some that were central to the mix that I had not yet thought of. I'm not concerned about it, because I have the right question: "How do I build a Mature Business, and when do I want to be there?" The right question is 90 percent of the answer. The other 10 percent is being manic about making sure you're getting it answered, which means I'm constantly improving on the answer as I go.

Remember Frodo and his journey into Mordor in Tolkien's Lord of the Rings trilogy? He had no idea how he was going to get to Mordor, but was very clear on the need to get there. For him there was no confusion about what the final result needed to be.

Most of us don't approach life like he did. Unfortunately we are more interested in fully understanding the process, than we are in even knowing the objective. We'll even give up knowing the end game as long as we don't have any surprises on our trip to nowhere.

The joy is in the journey, not in the destination.

I can tell you with conviction that the key is not figuring out the whole process in advance, but figuring out what Business Maturity looks like for you and exactly when you want to be there. If you know where you are going, you will figure out the process because the end game is so clear. What's your Mordor? Get that end game clear and, along with the next few steps, you'll be doing great.

• #16—Speed, Intentionality, Urgency, Vision

Businesses fail to grow up most often because we don't have Speed of Execution. We don't have Speed of Execution because we don't have Intentionality. We don't have Intentionality because we don't have a sense of Urgency tied to the Priority of the Impor-tant. We don't know what's

> Speed of Execution—the best indicator of success.

Important because we don't have Vision. We don't have a clue where in the world we're going, or when we want to be there. Clarity brings Hope, and Hope causes us to take the Risk to get moving. In the first few years of a business, Speed of Execution is the best indicator of Success. So get moving.

- ## #17—Conation

The only motivational book I will recommend to others is *Self-made in America* by John McClintock. John introduced me to an obscure English word that I now use as a building block for my daily activity: *conation.*

I've truncated John's working definition over the years to my own, which reads like this:

For a very long time now, psychologists have identified what they call the Three Aspects of the Mind: Cognition—the ability to think; Affection—the ability to feel; and this funny, obscure word Conation—the will and ability to do.

I find it fascinating that almost everyone I know has a good handle on what cognition and affection are, but virtually no one I know (including me until a number of years ago) has any idea that the third aspect of the mind is conation. Our educational system and our warped view of learning have promoted thinking and feeling almost to the exclusion of doing. There's very little work done on conation. Kathy Kolbe (*www.www.kolbe.com/*) has been the bright, shining light on conation and has kept us from losing this most valuable word.

> Conation—the will to succeed that manifests itself in single-minded pursuit of a goal.

I believe the reason this valuable word hasn't gotten much attention is because we have been trained to believe that we think our way to a new way of acting. We see cognition—thinking—as the all-important fundamental on which the other two swing. And of course we all like to feel stuff. So affection gets plenty of attention too.

But, we do not think our way to a new way of acting. We act our way to a new way of thinking.

Want to grow a Mature Business? Add "conate" to your daily verb count—the will to succeed that manifests itself in single-minded pursuit of a goal. Clarity—I know my goal; Hope—the will to succeed that comes from knowing my goal; and Risk—the single-minded pursuit—actually doing it.

It's all about intentionality. Let's look at it a different way. An Australian acquaintance of mine sat in my living room a number of years back and talked about ways of learning. He gave me a narrative for things I knew and practiced, but never really described it to myself other than in subconscious terms.

We don't think our way to a new way of acting. We act our way to a new way of thinking.

It is the act of doing that changes us, not the act of thinking. Thinking can prepare us to act, but when I get the ship moving and I move forward, I'm learning more than when I'm sitting around thinking about moving forward. Intentionality is very important. Yes, I said it again.

Get a reasonable idea of what you want to do, get as clear a picture as you can of what your Ideal Lifestyle looks like and what your business needs to look like to support that, put a date on it, go public, and get moving. Remember, the best indicator of success in early-stage business is not planning, research, product placement, marketing, sales, or refining the offering, but in speed of execution.

- ### #18—A Bad Plan in Motion Is Better Than a Good Plan Being Researched.

Lack of conation keeps us from moving forward. We're so busy cognating and affecting that we never get around to doing anything about it—always learning and never able to come to knowledge (action) of the truth.

Stop thinking about what you're doing. Cognition will not get you there. Stop waiting to feel good about it. Emotion is a terrible indicator of future success (it really only tells us about the past). Conate. Get a decent plan, make sure a few objective outsiders tell you you're not crazy, and go for it.

It's about commitment to executing your bad plan, not perfection of it. Get moving.

It is not how good your plan is that determines your success, but how committed you are to the bad plan you've got. As long as you know clearly where you want to go and when you want to be there, you'll figure out the process as you go.

Cognition demands that we understand the methodology and have the process clearly laid out before we begin. Conation demands that we know where we're going, when we want to get there, and that we start moving as quickly as possible toward that end. Do not stand around discussing where the bullets are coming from. Conate—get moving.

- ### #19—What If I Miss My Business Maturity Date? Have I failed?

If getting to your Business Maturity Date was your goal, then yes, you failed. But if getting to your Business Maturity Date is just a Waypoint along the way to living out your Lifetime Goals, then no. You simply adjust and keep moving, because the only thing that matters is getting to your Ideal Lifestyle so you can fully live out your Lifetime Goals.

Remember, Lifetime Goals can never be achieved in the traditional sense—you can never check them off as completed. As long as you have health and resources to do it, you can always work in your non-profit, travel, play with the grandchildren, work at being healthy and fit, impact the lives of others, and whatever else you feel will make for a life of significance for you.

If you set a Business Maturity Date four years out and on that day you're business isn't what you had pictured for Maturity, so what? The fact is you are much closer to that Waypoint simply by having the clarity to risk going for it. So what if you have to readjust and add six more months or a year to get there? So it took five years instead of four. If you hadn't tried to do it in four years, you'd be still mucking along on the treadmill in a Stage Four business thirty years later. How's that for failure?

> Random Hope is not a good business strategy. Get a Business Maturity Date.

I'll take the risk of arriving at my Business Maturity Date six months early or two years late over the Random Hope approach any day.

As we know, Random Hope is not a good business strategy, and the irony is that Random Hope leads to very certain failure. There is nothing random about the outcome. If you just dream about having a business that someday will support a lifestyle of significance, you're almost certainly never going to achieve it. Don't fear missing your Business Maturity Date—fear not having one.

- ## #20—Seven Decision-Making Principles Leading Us To Profitability

How we make decisions affects everything we do. Are you guiding your business or does it rule you? Are you simply reacting to shiny objects or leading your business with a simple strategic plan? Who's really in charge?

Like rails that guide a train, your decision-making principles are a core strategy to having a business that knows where it is going and how it is going to get there.

THE SEVEN DECISION-MAKING PRINCIPLES OF THE CRANKSET GROUP:

1. Business Maturity Date—Know where I'm going and when I want to get there.

2. Make more money in less time.

3. Focus on my lifetime goals, not just on growing my business.

4. Get off the treadmill, own the business instead of the business owning me.

5. Highest and best use of my time, work on, not just in my business.

6. Make decisions on where I want to be, not where I am.

7. Bad plans carried out violently many times yield good results. Do something. (My Marine Corps Soccer Team Motto—1980, and the subject of my next book.)

Here are my seven decision-making principles. What are yours?

What are the decision-making principles of your business?

You've got decision-making principles that are already running the show. You might as well write them down and see if you agree with who/what is actually in charge. If not, change them and take control of your business future.

• #21—Stuck in Neutral

The worst way to build a business or accomplish anything in life is to run away from something. People who focus on *not* being their alcoholic parent are more likely to become just like them. They're not running toward something, they're running away from something.

The best way to build a business and live a life of significance is to run madly toward something, to have a blue flame coming out your backside that says, "This one thing, I do." It's why I'm so crazy about you knowing your Lifetime Goals and your Business Maturity Date—so you can run madly toward something. People who live this way are almost always successful and the rest just get out of their way.

> If you don't have a vision for your own life, you'll become part of someone else's vision for theirs.

But the worst malady is to not be running away from or toward anything. To just be stuck in neutral. I've quoted John Heenan many times on this: If you don't have a vision for your own life, you'll become part of someone else's vision for theirs.

What are you running toward? And why?

• #22—Live a Disoriented Life

As I say to people attending my workshops and keynote addresses, I believe adults don't learn unless we're disoriented. We need to be shaken from our reality before we listen. Young kids learn all the time; they just soak it up because they are 100 percent confident they don't know everything yet. As we get older, we become confident we know things, and we stop learning.

Be sure of very few things. Live a disoriented life.

When I started taking golf lessons, I had already been working at it and reading books about it for a few years, so I figured I was at least 20 percent of the way to knowing golf. After a year of lessons I was sure I knew no more than 5 percent, and the number was falling fast.

Be sure of very few things. Live a disoriented life.

GETTING THERE

Stephen Lipscomb, a client of mine, decided at the age of 25 that he would retire at the age of 50 with $6 million in the bank. At the age of 50, he had the $6 million and retired. The next year he lost everything in the real estate crash of 2008. Utterly devastated, he came to me to find out how to pick up the pieces and start all over again. He was very depressed, had trouble doing work while he was at the office, and most days simply went home by 1 p.m.

Stephen was just treading water and at a complete loss as to how he could ever get back on track. It had taken 25 years to amass his small fortune, and the thought of working as hard for another 25 years until he was 75 was suffocating. Everything he had worked for and achieved had vanished. His life was an empty shell, and he was a mere shadow of his former self.

But why? What was the real issue? Was it that it takes 25 years to accumulate enough money to enjoy life? I don't think so. The root of Stephen's present depression was that he had decided (intended) that it would take 25 years to do it the first time, and it did. So he had proved to himself that it would take another 25 to get there the second time, and being 75 before he arrived was too much to bear.

I'm not a big proponent of "positive thinking" because too often it gets disconnected from positive action, positive skill development, positive discipline, and diligence. But I believe the biggest reason Stephen was seeing the future as hopeless was his own intentionality—both in the past and in the future. He had intended to take 25 years to finish working, and he did. So his assumption going forward was that it would take the same amount of time and effort. And it would. Because he believed it would.

We get what we intend. Sure, there are outside forces at play that speed up or slow down the process, but we almost always end up in the ball park of what we intend to achieve. But much more important than arriving where we intend to arrive, we almost always get there *when* we decide to get there.

Why do most people retire at 60 to 70 years old? Because that is exactly what they intended to do. It has nothing to do with it taking that long to accumulate what you need to live a significant, meaningful, and rich life. Most people take 30 to 40 years to get it done because they never intended to do anything else.

And lack of any choice at all is still a choice. By default we choose to take 30 to 40 years and yet still never grow a Mature Business. We regularly become part of someone else's vision for their lives because we didn't have one for ourselves. Are you being dragged along by the Tyranny of the Urgent or are you grabbing the Priority of the Important by the horns and creating a significant future for yourself?

HOW TO CREATE YOUR FUTURE

How do you steer a ship? You might be surprised to know it is not by moving the rudder. It's by moving the ship. The rudder won't turn the ship unless the ship is moving. And the faster the ship is moving, the less you have to move the rudder to make a significant impact on the direction of the ship.

Your dream won't become a vision by thinking, planning, researching, hoping, wishing, and waiting for the right time to move. There is no right time and there is no such thing as a good plan—they're all bad as soon as the world starts beating them up. Make a decision and get moving. The movement will give you the feedback to turn your bad plan into a good one.

What if Steven decided to take four years this next time? Could a guy who built $6 million in personal riches in 25 years do it in four or five? Of course he can, especially since he's already done it once. But first he will have to make the following adjustment: Rather than seeing himself as a mere shadow of his *former* self, he'll have to see himself as my friend Donald McGilchrist sees himself:

"I am a mere shadow of my *future* self."

Stephen is focused on what he lost, and what he can't do going forward. Until he gets a clear picture of a new way of thinking, he'll intend to not rebuild what he once had.

What are you intending to do?

Are you intending to accumulate riches that you don't have time to use, or build a life of significance and use your business to get you there? If you focus on the Tyranny of the Urgent, you will at best make money (never as much as you could otherwise).

If you focus on the Priority of the Important, you're on the road to real Wealth. But since we can't see a way that these "Important" things will make us money today, we always find a way to put off dealing with them until later. But later never comes. Make a decision when your business will be mature, put a date on it, and go public.

It's not about one business owner being more talented than the next or having better circumstances then you have. It's about intentionality.

Remember our definition of wealth: *The freedom and the ability to choose what to do with my time.* Build a business that makes money without you being the producer so you can build a life of significance for yourself and those in your world. And do it in three to five years.

An After Word
For Going Forward

Using Your Business to Build a Life of Significance

believe we all have a natural desire to be significant and to be contributing members of society. Yet few of us truly feel like we are creating the rules that will allow us to succeed. One way to escape from this in today's world is to live our lives through other people via reality TV, gurus, experts, music groups, sports stars, business experts and other heroes.

Rather than encouraging us to do and be the same, this constant focus on "exceptional people" can keep us from building our own life of significance. We feel if our sports hero wins, we win. Or if my business guru is paying attention to me, I'm significant. While we idolize our hero, too often we lose sight of what got them there. And I can guarantee you that with very few exceptions, it wasn't talent, but struggle.

Is it possible that deep commitment to the effort it takes to get to your Big Why is what actually creates meaning and joy?

Are we too focused on the result, thinking that "arriving" will make us happy? Why do athletes, music heroes, and business people who are already at the top of their field and financially secure keep going? Why don't they retire as soon as they get there?

I believe it is because they have found the secret (such an over used term) of meaning and joy. They understand that joy is not found in the destination but in the journey, and that love of the process of persistent struggle is the key to joy.

How did your star athlete get to the level they are at? By persistent struggle on the weight machines, on the track and daily work at perfecting their craft. Relentless, consistent, persistent struggle. And a deep love for that process. Yo Yo Ma (world-famous cellist) once told my daughter "The key to becoming a world class musician is to learn to love to practice; to practice every day as if you're sitting on stage at Carnegie Hall for your debut concert."

Do you love the process or are you focused on the result? Measure the result, but focus on the process, and learn to love the process of building your mental muscles. Learn to love the process and the ongoing development of both your craft and your business. You will find the most meaning and joy in having made it through the tough times and having created success by loving the persistent process of getting there.

> Joy is not found in the destination but in the journey.

Your heroes didn't get there by talent. They got there by learning to love the process of getting there. Take the things in this book with you into the real world, get beat up, fall down, get back up a little stronger, and do it again. Build your mental muscles one at a time, but relentlessly. Unswerving commitment to the process of getting there is the only thing that will get you there. We get what we intend, not what we hope for.

Circumstances don't make me who I am. How I respond to them does.

Respond with tenacity! That will get you there! Do what it takes to build a business and a life of significance!

Let's do it together!

Resources

Following are examples of three workshops and seminars that have been received with rave reviews in a number of US states and countries of the world:

No-Nonsense Strategic Plan Workshop
It's time to trade in that worthless, dusty Business Plan for a Strategic Plan that will:

- guide you tactically/practically every day (a rolling 12-month plan)
- make it easy to measure if each week/month/quarter is making you money
- be concise and clear enough you could stand and share your annual strategy in 2-3 minutes.

Develop a Strategic Plan right in the workshop to run your business daily and get it to Maturity.

Strategic Plan online

As of the writing of this book we are working on developing an online Strategic Plan application. If you would like to be notified when it is completed, please visit:

www.cranksetgroup.com
or e-mail us at grow@cranksetgroup.com.

This will also qualify you for a significantly reduced cost if you choose to use the Strategic Plan online application.

No-Nonsense Process Mapping— The Key to a Great Business
Dive into this workshop and find out exactly how to:

- Identify and shift to the highest and best use of your time—stop guessing—make more money in less time.
- Deliver the same great level of customer service every time to every customer, easily.
- Create ownership and teamwork where none existed before—get rid of the "job silos" problem.
- Make your company worth exponentially more if you ever wanted to sell it.

Process Mapping online

As of the writing of this book we are working on developing an online Process Mapping application. If you would like to be in a beta group or be notified when it is completed, please visit:

www.cranksetgroup.com
or e-mail us at grow@cranksetgroup.com.

This will also qualify you for a significantly reduced cost if you choose to use the Strategic Plan online application.

No-Nonsense Lifetime Goals
for Business People

- How do you define Success and Significance? Why are you in business? Where is it taking you?
- *What* does your Ideal Lifestyle look like? *When* do you expect to get there? *How* will your business get you there?

You will get a clear picture and a new motivation on how your business can get you where you want to be.

Lifetime Goals online

In early 2011 we will be developing an online version of this workshop. We would love your input. And if you would like to be in a beta group or notified when it is completed, please visit:

www.cranksetgroup.com
or e-mail us at grow@cranksetgroup.com.

This will also qualify you for a significantly reduced cost if you choose to use the Strategic Plan online application.

The Apex Profile online

The profiles you saw in Chapter Nine are available online right now. If you want to take the Apex Profile online e-mail the author at grow@cranksetgroup.com and request a one-time code be sent to you for the Profile, which you will find at www.apexprofile.com. This code will reduce the cost of the profile to only $10.00. You can visit www.apexprofile.com for more information.

About the Author

Chuck Blakeman is a lifetime business practitioner who now uses his experience to help business owners create success. He speaks and works with businesses in the U.S., Europe, Africa, and Australasia. His company, The Crankset Group, provides outcome-based mentoring, peer advisory, and consulting for Business Owners, CEOs, and their growing businesses.

Mr. Blakeman began his career in the U.S. Army, followed by 13 years service in non-profit leadership development. He started and grew five small businesses, including one sold to the largest consumer fulfillment company in America. He helped lead three other companies between $20-$100 million through repositioning in the Marketing Support Services industry.

Mr. Blakeman is considered a thought leader in the Marketing Support Services industry and has decades of experience in sales, marketing and operations of companies involved in branding, database and website development, call centers, fulfillment, printing and direct mail processing.

Some of Mr. Blakeman's customers have included Microsoft, Apple, Eli Lilly, TAP Pharmaceuticals, Sun Microsystems, Tyco Healthcare, Johns Manville and many more.

He is a regular convention speaker, magazine contributor, and non-profit board member. His new book, *"Making Money is Killing Your Business"* is radically changing the way business owners understand growth. Recent appearances include Entrepreneur Magazine, CNNMoney.com, NYTimes.com, Bizjournals.com, CoBiz Magazine, Home Business Magazine, keynote speaker at MFSA/Maui, and many others.

Chuck is available for one2one advising, conference workshops and seminars to help business owners make more money in less time and get back to the passion that brought them into business in the first place.

BUSINESS ADVISORY, SPEAKING, SEMINARS AND WORKSHOPS

To discuss possible business engagements with Chuck, please visit:

www.cranksetgroup.com or e-mail the author at

grow@cranksetgroup.com